Bookkeeping and Accounting In A Week

Roger Mason is a Chartered Certified Accountant with many years' practical experience as a Finance Director at a number of leading companies. He now lectures on financial and business topics. In addition, he has edited a financial publication and written many books.

Bookkeeping and Accounting In A Week

Teach Yourself®

Roger Mason

First published in Great Britain in 1995 by Hodder & Stoughton. An Hachette UK company.

This revised, updated edition published by John Murray Learning 2016.

This edition published in the US in 2016 by Quercus.

British Library Cataloguing in Publication Data: a catalogue record for this title is available from the British Library.

Library of Congress Catalog Card Number: on file.

Paperback ISBN 978 1473 60769 9

Ebook ISBN 978 1 4441 5876 2

1

The publisher has used its best endeavours to ensure that any website addresses referred to in this book are correct and active at the time of going to press. However, the publisher and the author have no responsibility for the websites and can make no guarantee that a site will remain live or that the content will remain relevant, decent or appropriate.

The publisher has made every effort to mark as such all words which it believes to be trademarks. The publisher should also like to make it clear that the presence of a word in the book, whether marked or unmarked, in no way affects its legal status as a trademark.

Every reasonable effort has been made by the publisher to trace the copyright holders of material in this book. Any errors or omissions should be notified in writing to the publisher, who will endeavour to rectify the situation for any reprints and future editions.

Typeset by Cenveo® Publisher Services.

Printed and bound in Great Britain by CPI Group (UK) Ltd., Croydon, CR0 4YY.

John Murray Learning policy is to use papers that are natural, renewable and recyclable products and made from wood grown in sustainable forests. The logging and manufacturing processes are expected to conform to the environmental regulations of the country of origin.

John Murray Learning
Carmelite House
50 Victoria Embankment
London EC4Y 0DZ
www.hodder.co.uk

Also available in ebook

Contents

Introduction

Millions of sets of accounting records are kept in Britain and around the world. They range from the accounts of major companies employing tens or hundreds of thousands of people to the cashbook of small local bodies such as a stamp collectors' club or tennis club. An understanding of the principles of bookkeeping and accounts is of great importance, and not just to people employed in accounts offices. Depending on how far you are willing to stretch the definition, there are well over a million non-financial managers in Britain, with considerably more in other countries. A knowledge of the subjects covered in this book will help them do their jobs and progress in their careers.

It is probably true to say that such knowledge is more important now than ever before. With this basic understanding, you will be able to deal effectively with such questions as:

- Sales are up! How can there possibly be an overdraft?
- Why does every bookkeeping entry have two sides?
- What is the accountant talking about?
- Just what is a contingency account?

Of course, it is not only at work that some knowledge of bookkeeping and accounting is useful. Many good-natured people struggle with the books of clubs and such bodies as parent–teachers' organizations. Often they do a good job, but sometimes they do not.

This book is written for anyone wishing to master these principles, whether or not they are a manager. By setting aside a little time each day for a week, you should develop the necessary understanding.

Most bookkeeping and accounting is now done with computers. This has enormous advantages but it may result in people using them without understanding what they are doing. These accounting packages do follow the old-established and time-honoured principles explained in this book, so this book should help you understand what the computers are doing.

Please note that your learning on Saturday will be more effective if you have a company's Annual Report and Accounts to hand. It would be helpful if you could obtain this in advance.

The book contains 70 multiple-choice questions, the correct answers to which are given at the end of the book. I do hope that you attempt them. A score of 60 is good and anything higher is exceptional.

I want you to start in a good mood, so I will ask how you can tell if a person is an accountant. My son, who like me is an accountant, says that you can tell because accountants are introverts and will look at your shoes rather than look you in the eye. The only people more introverted than accountants are actuaries. They look at their own shoes rather than yours!

I have enjoyed writing this book and I hope that you enjoy reading it or, at the very least, find it useful. My best wishes for your future success.

Roger Mason

SUNDAY

The basic principles of bookkeeping

Today we start by looking at the foundations of bookkeeping. As with so many things, our end results will be far better if we lay the foundations correctly. As Julie Andrews famously sang in *The Sound of Music*, 'Let's start at the very beginning, a very good place to start.'

Millions of sets of accounting records are kept in a huge range of contexts. At one extreme, scores of qualified accountants toil to prepare the published accounts of a major company. At the other extreme, the treasurer of a local tennis club or PTA reports on the finances to the members.

All the records, from the mightiest to the most humble, should be kept according to the basic principles of bookkeeping. These are timeless and the same for all organizations. A study of basic principles is an excellent way of starting the week.

We will look at:

- single-entry bookkeeping
- the concept of double-entry bookkeeping
- the basic rules and disciplines of double-entry bookkeeping.

Single-entry bookkeeping

As the name suggests, single-entry bookkeeping involves writing down each transaction just once. It is, in fact, the simple listing of income and expenditure. Numerous small organizations – such as your local tennis club, for example – will keep their records in this way.

Every time the treasurer writes a cheque, he or she records in a book the date, the amount and the payee. Every time something is paid into the bank, the details are entered elsewhere in the book. Cash paid out or received is entered in a similar way.

If the treasurer has been careful, he or she can use these records to prepare an accurate receipts and payments account. It is necessary, however, to prove the figures as far as possible. Cash actually in the cash box should equal the cash received less the cash paid out, after allowing for the starting balance, of course. The balance on the bank statement should equal money banked less cheques written, after allowing for the opening balance and items that have not yet reached the statement.

Records kept in this way have severe limitations, including the following.

● An item written down wrongly may not be noticed as a mistake.

- Money owing to the organization or by the organization is not shown. The tennis club accounts will not show subscriptions not paid by members, or the amount owing to a painter for painting the clubhouse.
- Long-term assets are not shown: for example, £1,000 spent on tennis nets last year is not shown in the current year's accounts.

Double-entry bookkeeping

The concept and principles of double-entry bookkeeping were first written down in 1494 by an Italian monk named Luca Pacioli. His work has stood the test of time – the same principles are still valid today.

At the heart of double-entry bookkeeping is the idea that every transaction involves the giving of a benefit and the receiving of a benefit. Consequently, every transaction is written into the books twice, once as a credit and once as a debit.

It follows from this that the bookkeeping system must balance, which is an enormous advantage for control purposes. The total of the debits must equal the total of the credits.

A set of double-entry books enables a complete view to be taken, unlike a single-entry system. For example, consider a businessperson writing out a cheque for £100 wages. In a single-entry system the only information recorded is that £100 wages has been paid. A double-entry system also records that £100 has been taken from the bank account and that the bank account balance is reduced accordingly. This is extremely important information.

The basic rules and disciplines of double-entry bookkeeping

A manual ledger or account is ruled for posting on two sides. Young trainee accountants were customarily told on their first morning that debit is nearest the window. Of course, this is only true if they work with their left shoulders to the glass. Here are the basic rules:

1 Debit on the left, credit on the right

Computerized records are not likely to be printed in this traditional way. You are more likely to get a printout showing columns of figures. Some of these figures represent credits and some represent debits. They could be rewritten in the traditional format, though, and the debits would go on the left.

2 For every debit there must be a credit

This is another rule customarily told to trainee accountants on their first morning. Unlike the advice about windows, this rule is infallible. There are no exceptions. Let us return to the businessperson writing out a cheque for £100 wages. The entries are:

| Wages account | £100.00 debit |
| Bank account | £100.00 credit |

The entries may be numerous and complicated, but the rule still holds. If it is not followed, the trial balance will not balance. A mistake has been made which must be found and corrected. Let us take the businessperson purchasing £100 stationery which carries 20% recoverable VAT. The entries are:

Stationery account	£100.00 debit
VAT account	£20.00 debit
Bank account	£120.00 credit

Scientists sometimes help themselves to remember the rule by thinking of the law of physics 'For every action there is an equal and opposite reaction.'

3 Debit receives the benefit, credit gives the benefit

This may be hard to grasp and it is probably the opposite of what you would instinctively expect. After all, your bank statement is credited when it receives money paid in. Nevertheless, double-entry bookkeeping does work in this way. An account is debited when it receives a benefit and it is credited when it gives a benefit.

Consider again the businessperson writing out a cheque for £100 wages. The worker receives the money and it is the wages account that is debited. The bank account gives the benefit and, as a result, has less money in it. Consequently, the bank account is credited.

It may help you to remember the rule if you think that a bank overdraft is represented by a credit balance in the bookkeeping system.

For another example we will take a sale of £200 to Smith and Sons. If it is a cash sale, the entry is:

Bank account	£200.00 debit
Sales account	£200.00 credit

Money has been paid into the bank and the bank account is debited. If it is a sale on credit, the entry is:

Smith and Sons   £200.00 debit
Sales account   £200.00 credit

When Smith and Sons actually pay, the entry is:

Bank account   £200.00 debit
Smith and Sons   £200.00 credit

The best way of understanding the basic principles is to work through examples, and two are given here. In the first case the correct entries follow immediately. In the second example just the account headings are given. You should fill in the entries before checking the correct postings, which are given at the end of today's work.

1 Samantha Jones runs a ladies' dress shop

On one day the following events occur:

- She banks cash takings of £460.
- She makes a credit sale of £100 to Mrs Clarke.
- She purchases dresses from London Dress Supplies for £1,000. This is on credit.
- She pays wages of £110.
- Mrs Clarke pays £80 owing from a previous sale. This is banked.

Bank account

Debit			Credit	
	£			£
Sales account	460	Wages account		110
Mrs Clarke account	80			

Sales account

Debit			Credit	
	£			£
		Bank account		100
		Mrs Clarke account		460

Mrs Clarke account

Debit			Credit	
	£			£
Sales account	100	Bank account		80

Stock account

Debit			Credit	
	£			£
London Dress Supplies account	1,000			

London Dress Supplies account

Debit			Credit	
	£			£
		Stock account		1,000

Wages account

Debit			Credit	
	£			£
Bank account	110			

The layout of the accounts has been simplified because only the principles of posting are being illustrated. In real life each entry would be dated and the balance of each account would be shown. Note that the total of all the debits equals the total of all the credits, i.e. £1,750 in each case.

2 Peter Jenkins starts a manufacturing business

- He pays £50,000 into the bank as his capital for the business.
- He buys plant and machinery for £20,000 from King Brothers Ltd. This is on credit.
- He buys raw materials from Patel Brothers for £10,000. This is on credit.
- He buys raw materials for £6,000 for cash.
- He pays his lawyer £2,000 for negotiating a lease.

Now test your understanding by filling in the entries on the following blank accounts table. You can check the answers at the end of today's work.

Accounts table

Bank account

Debit		Credit
£		£

Capital account

Debit		Credit
£		£

Plant and machinery account

Debit		Credit
£		£

King Brothers Ltd account

Debit		Credit
£		£

Patel Brothers Ltd account

Debit		Credit
£		£

Raw materials account

Debit		Credit
£		£

Legal and professional account

Debit		Credit
£		£

Summary

Today we have learned the basic principles of bookkeeping, and laid the foundations of our understanding. We have:

- looked at single-entry records and seen the drawbacks
- established what is meant by double-entry and seen the advantages
- seen that the giving and receiving of a benefit is at the heart of double-entry bookkeeping
- gained an understanding of the basic rules and principles
- worked through two examples.

Tomorrow we will establish the five different types of account. We will also examine the different ledgers and day books.

Test your understanding

Answer

Accounts table

Bank account

Debit	£		Credit	£
Capital account	50,000	Raw materials account		6,000
		Legal and professional account		2,000

Capital account

Debit	£		Credit	£
		Bank account		50,000

Plant and Machinery account

Debit	£		Credit	£
King Brothers Ltd account	20,000			

King Brothers Ltd account

Debit	£		Credit	£
		Plant and machinery account		20,000

Patel Brothers Ltd account

Debit	£		Credit	£
		Raw materials account		10,000

Raw Materials account

Debit	£		Credit	£
Patel Brothers Ltd account	10,000			
Bank account	6,000			

Legal and Professional account

Debit	£		Credit	£
Bank account	2,000			

Fact-check (answers at the back)

1. Which of the following is a disadvantage of single-entry bookkeeping?
   a) An asset purchased last year is not shown in this year's accounts ❑
   b) It takes more time than double-entry bookkeeping ❑
   c) It is against the law ❑
   d) It is not usually explained in accounting textbooks ❑

2. Who first wrote down the principles of double-entry bookkeeping?
   a) Salvador Dalí ❑
   b) Roy Salvadori ❑
   c) Luca Pacioli ❑
   d) Silvio Berlusconi ❑

3. Which of the following are features of double-entry bookkeeping?
   a) Every transaction is entered twice, once as a credit and once as a debit ❑
   b) The bookkeeping system must balance ❑
   c) The total of the debits must equal the total of the credits ❑
   d) All of the above ❑

4. Complete the following. For every debit there must be a...
   a) Debt ❑
   b) Credit ❑
   c) Loss ❑
   d) Problem ❑

5. Where in a manual ledger does debit go?
   a) At the top ❑
   b) At the bottom ❑
   c) On the left ❑
   d) On the right ❑

6. What happens in the bookkeeping system when a cheque for £600 is written?
   a) Nothing happens until the bank pays the cheque ❑
   b) Bank account is debited £600 ❑
   c) Bank account is credited £600 ❑
   d) Sales are debited £600 ❑

7. What happens in the bookkeeping system when cash takings of £600 are banked?
   a) Bank account is debited £600 ❑
   b) Sales account is credited £600 ❑
   c) Both (a) and (b) above ❑
   d) Nothing ❑

8. A sale of £600 is made on credit to Banerjee Brothers Ltd. Which account is debited?
   a) Bank account ❑
   b) Banerjee Brothers Ltd ❑
   c) Sales ❑
   d) Stock ❑

9. A sale of £600 is made on credit to Banerjee Brothers Ltd. Which account is credited?
a) Bank account ❏
b) Banerjee Brothers Ltd ❏
c) Sales ❏
d) Stock ❏

10. Which of the following statements is correct?
a) Double-entry bookkeeping is far superior to single-entry bookkeeping ❏
b) Double-entry bookkeeping is slightly superior to single-entry bookkeeping ❏
c) Double-entry bookkeeping is slightly inferior to single-entry bookkeeping ❏
d) Double-entry bookkeeping is much inferior to single-entry bookkeeping ❏

MONDAY

Different types of account and ledger

The rules for posting between accounts follow the rules of double-entry bookkeeping. They do not vary according to the types of account involved. However, different types of account fulfil different purposes. They are treated differently when the profit and loss account and balance sheet are prepared.

We start today by looking at the five different types of account. We then progress to an examination of the nominal ledger, together with the subsidiary ledgers and the books of entry.

The programme is:

- the five different types of account
- the nominal ledger
- the sales ledger
- the sales day book
- the purchase ledger
- the purchases day book.

The five different types of account

It will be helpful for you to have an understanding of the different types of account. This is in order to understand the books and it is very important when accounts are prepared. We will see this later in the week. However, it does not affect the bookkeeping, and postings may freely be made from one type of account to another.

Income accounts

These accounts relate to sales and they increase the profit. The income accounts normally have a credit balance and are eventually credited to the profit and loss account. An example is the sales account into which Samantha Jones credited £460 in Sunday's first example.

Expenditure accounts

These accounts are made up of expenditure that reduces profit. The expenditure accounts normally have a debit balance and are eventually debited to the profit and loss account. An example of an expenditure account is the wages account with a £110 balance from Sunday's first example.

Asset accounts

These accounts normally have a debit balance and are made up of assets that retain their value. This is distinct from, say, the electricity account, which is an expenditure account. Examples of asset accounts are stock, motor vehicles, and bank accounts with no overdraft. Money owing to the business is in debtor accounts and these are asset accounts. An example is Mrs Clarke's account in Sunday's first example. Asset accounts go into the balance sheet, not the profit and loss account.

Liability accounts

These accounts are the debts of the business and they normally have a credit balance. They eventually go into the balance sheet, not the profit and loss account. Examples are the accounts for money owing to suppliers and these accounts are called creditors. A further example is the bank account if there is an overdraft.

Capital accounts

These accounts represent the investment in the business by the owners. If the business is a company, it is the net worth owned by the shareholders. If you refer back to Sunday's second example, you will see that Peter Jenkins started his business by paying in £50,000, and that this was credited to a capital account. If the business makes profits, the value of the capital accounts will increase in time.

So long as a business is solvent, the capital accounts will have credit balances. If a business is not solvent, the capital accounts will have debit balances. This is a sign of desperate trouble and often means that the closing of the business is imminent.

Test your understanding

Now test your understanding of the types of account by classifying the following list. The answers are given at the end of today's work, but write them down before checking.

Write the type of account and whether the balances are normally debit or credit.

	Type of account	Debit or credit?
1 Fixtures and fittings account	Asset	Debit
2 Salaries account	Expenditure	Debit
3 Legal and professional expenses account	Expenditure	Debit
4 Revenue reserves account	Capital	Credit
5 Share capital account	Capital	Credit
6 Trade debtors account	Asset	Debit
7 Trade creditors account	Liabilitie	credit
8 Hire purchase creditors account	Liabilitied	Credit
9 Shop takings account	Income	Credit
10 Goods sold account	Income	Credit

The nominal ledger

The nominal ledger is the principal ledger. If other ledgers are kept, they reconcile to a control account within the nominal ledger.

In very simple accounting systems only one ledger is maintained (the nominal ledger) and every single account is part of this main ledger. If there are, say, ten customers, each one has an account within the nominal ledger. This option is open to all but it is practical only in the case of small and simple systems. Sheer numbers often necessitate the keeping of subsidiary sales and purchase ledgers. The detailed sales and purchase ledgers each reconcile to their own control account within the nominal ledger. According to circumstances, other subsidiary ledgers may be kept. An example is a listing of the various fixed asset accounts.

The nominal ledger may be very big, perhaps containing thousands of individual accounts. This will certainly be the case for a major company and it is therefore necessary to have a system for coding and grouping the accounts.

In a simple system the accounts will just be listed, probably in alphabetical order. In a more complex system they will be grouped in a logical manner. For example, if there are several bank accounts, they may be listed next to each other. This is convenient and, when the balance sheet is prepared, all the bank accounts will be added to the one total that will appear in it. Similarly, it is usual to group all the overhead expenditure accounts by department.

In all but the very smallest systems it is normal to give each account an identifying number. This is quicker to write out and, if the system is mechanized or computerized, the person posting the entries will post according to the numbers only.

Numbering systems

There are thousands of different accounting numbering systems and you may want to design your own to fit your business and individual circumstances. It is worth looking at the numbering system of your employer or some other organization. Whether or not it is a good system, make sure that you understand the principles of the numbering.

The sales ledger

If your business is so specialized that you have only one customer, you will not need a detailed sales ledger, just one account in the nominal ledger. And you will not need a sales ledger if your sales are entirely for cash.

On the other hand, most businesses that sell on credit will have many customers. For them, an efficient sales ledger outside the nominal ledger is essential.

A manual sales ledger account looks very like a nominal ledger account. It is divided in the middle with debit on the left and credit on the right. There will be one account for each customer and the postings to it are as shown below.

Manual sales ledger	
Debit	Invoices issued
Credit	Credit notes issued
Credit	Cash received
Credit	Invoices written off as bad debts

Normally, the debits on each account will exceed the credits. This means that the account has a debit balance, which is the amount owed to the business by the customer. The total of the balances of all the sales ledger accounts is equal to the total amount owed to the business by the customers. This sum is represented by just one account (usually called the sales ledger control account) in the nominal system.

TIP

The bookkeeping system is designed to ensure that the accounts in the sales ledger do actually add up to the balance of the control account.

You will rarely encounter sales ledger accounts ruled in the traditional way described, although some small businesses may still use them. You will probably only be familiar with computer printouts that do not look anything like the ledgers described. It is important to remember, though, that a computer is just an efficient way of doing what could be done manually.

Some of the figures on the computer printout will represent credits and some will represent debits. They are just presented differently from a manual ledger. It is worth proving this to yourself by marking the debits and credits on a computerized sales ledger.

A business needs to send out statements and operate credit control procedures. These are a by-product of the sales ledgers; a computerized system simply speeds up the process. A computerized system may operate on the open item principle. This means that cash payments are allocated to specific invoices, and customer statements only show unpaid

invoices. A computerized system may readily give useful management information, such as an ageing of the debts.

The sales day book

It is necessary to have a mechanism for posting sales invoices into the sales ledger and the nominal ledger. This could be done laboriously one by one, but it is better to group them together and cut down the work.

This posting medium is usually called the sales day book, although you might find it called the sales journal or some other name. The following is a typical example of a sales day book. However, the design can vary according to individual preference and business circumstances.

Date	Customer	Invoice no.	Folio no.	Goods total £	VAT £	Invoice total £
1 June	Bigg and Son	1001	B4	100.00	20.00	120.00
4 June	Carter Ltd	1002	C1	200.00	40.00	240.00
12 June	XYZ Ltd	1003	X1	50.00	10.00	60.00
17 June	Martin Bros	1004	M2	100.00	20.00	120.00
26 June	Fishers Ltd	1005	F5	10.00	2.00	12.00
30 June	Dawson Ltd	1006	D2	20.00	4.00	24.00
				480.00	96.00	576.00

Please note the following about the columns:

- *Date* This is the date of each individual invoice.
- *Customer* This is the customer to whom each individual invoice is addressed.
- *Invoice no.* Each invoice must be individually numbered.
- *Folio no.* This is the identifying code to each individual sales ledger account.
- *Goods total* This is the total value of each invoice excluding VAT. Sometimes this is further divided to include different totals for different product groups. The example given shows only total sales.
- *VAT* This is the VAT charged on each individual invoice.
- *Invoice total* This is the total amount of each individual invoice and the amount that the customer has to pay.

The columns may be added and the posting done whenever it is convenient to do so. Monthly posting is frequently encountered and, in practice, there are likely to be more than six invoices. The posting to the nominal ledger would be:

Sales account	£480.00 credit	The sales account will eventually contribute to profit in the profit and loss account.
VAT account	£96.00 credit	This is a liability account. It is money owed by the business to the government.
Sales ledger control account	£576.00 debit	This is an asset account. It is money owing to the business by customers.

Six individual sales ledger accounts are debited with the total amount of the six individual invoices. You will notice that the balances of the sales ledger accounts will add up to the value of the sales ledger control account in the nominal system.

If you have a computerized system, your records will probably not look like this example. The computer will follow exactly these principles and do the same job, but it will do it much more quickly.

The purchase ledger

If you have thoroughly understood the section on the sales ledger, you will have no trouble understanding this section on the purchase ledger. This is because the purchase ledger is a mirror image of the sales ledger. It is used for invoices submitted to the business by suppliers.

The layout is similar to the accounts in the nominal ledger and the sales ledger. Postings to it are as shown below.

Purchase ledger	
Credit	Suppliers' invoices received
Debit	Suppliers' credit notes received
Debit	Cash payments made

Each account will normally have a credit balance and this represents the amount owing to the supplier by the business. The total of all the individual purchase ledger accounts is the same as the amount of the purchase ledger control account in the nominal ledger. Customers will submit statements to you and press you to make regular prompt payments to them.

The purchases day book

We have already seen that the purchase ledger is a mirror image of the sales ledger. You will therefore not be surprised to learn that the purchases day book is a mirror image of the sales day book. Do not be confused if you find it called the purchases journal or some other name, and do not be confused if it is a computerized system with a layout that makes sense to computer experts.

A typical purchase day book looks like the following:

Date	Customer	Invoice no.	Folio no.	Goods total £	VAT £	Invoice total £
1 July	Jones Ltd	3001	J8	100.00	20.00	120.00
9 July	King and Co	3002	K3	300.00	60.00	360.00
13 July	ABC Ltd	3003	A1	50.00	10.00	60.00
20 July	Dodd & Carr	3004	D2	200.00	40.00	240.00
28 July	Sugar Co Ltd	3005	S8	30.00	6.00	36.00
				680.00	136.00	816.00

The purchases day book is the medium through which a batch of suppliers' invoices is posted into the nominal system and into the purchase ledger. It avoids the need to enter them individually into the nominal system. It is usually ruled off and entered monthly but you can do this at any suitable interval.

Test your understanding

Now test your understanding by writing down the three nominal posting entries resulting from the above purchases day book. Also write down the balance of Jones Ltd in the purchase ledger. The answers are given at the end of today's work.

Summary

Today we have understood the five different types of nominal account and the differences between them. We have had a detailed look at:

- the nominal ledger
- the sales ledger
- the sales day book
- the purchase ledger
- the purchases day book.

Tomorrow we will continue our study of different aspects of bookkeeping.

Test your understanding

Answers

Types of account

1	Assets account	normally debit balance
2	Expenditure account	normally debit balance
3	Expenditure account	normally debit balance
4	Capital account	normally credit balance
5	Capital account	normally credit balance
6	Assets account	normally debit balance
7	Liabilities account	normally credit balance
8	Liabilities account	normally credit balance
9	Income account	normally credit balance
10	Income account	normally credit balance

Nominal postings

Purchases account	£680.00 debit
VAT account	£136.00 debit
Purchase ledger control account	£816.00 credit

In practice, the £680.00 would probably be spread over several different purchases account.

Jones Ltd will have a credit balance of £120.00 in the purchase ledger.

Fact-check (answers at the back)

1. Where are income accounts eventually credited?
   a) The balance sheet ❑
   b) The profit and loss account ❑
   c) The fixed assets ❑
   d) The directors' report ❑

2. What conclusion would you draw if the capital accounts have an overall debit balance?
   a) The bookkeeper has made a mistake ❑
   b) There has been a loss in the current year ❑
   c) The business is insolvent ❑
   d) The shareholders have not paid for their shares ❑

3. Which *two* of the following may be credited to a sales ledger account?
   a) Invoices issued ❑
   b) Credit notes issued ❑
   c) Cash received ❑
   d) Cash returned to the customer ❑

4. What does it mean if a sales ledger account has a debit balance?
   a) The customer owes money to the business ❑
   b) The business owes money to the customer ❑
   c) Deliveries have not yet reached the customer ❑
   d) Orders are still outstanding ❑

5. What does the sales day book do?
   a) It tells you the total sales for each day ❑
   b) It is the posting medium for sales invoices ❑
   c) It lists the credit balances in the bookkeeping system ❑
   d) It lists the debit balances in the bookkeeping system ❑

6. To what must the balances of the sales ledger accounts add up?
   a) The total sales ❑
   b) The profit ❑
   c) The assets ❑
   d) The balance of the sales ledger control account ❑

7. What does it mean if a purchase ledger account has a debit balance?
   a) The supplier owes money to the business ❑
   b) The business owes money to the supplier ❑
   c) Deliveries have not yet reached the business ❑
   d) A mistake has been made ❑

8. What is the purchases day book a mirror of?
   a) The sales day book ❑
   b) The purchase ledger ❑
   c) The sales ledger ❑
   d) None of the above ❑

9. When can the purchases day book be ruled off and entered?
a) Weekly ❏
b) Monthly ❏
c) Yearly ❏
d) Any convenient time ❏

10. What sort of account is stock?
a) Income ❏
b) Expenditure ❏
c) Capital ❏
d) Assets ❏

TUESDAY

More aspects of bookkeeping

On Sunday and Monday we examined the basic foundations of bookkeeping and keeping different types of account and different ledgers. Today we will build on that work by looking at more aspects of bookkeeping. We must do this before we can move on to preparatory work for the accounts. This, and the accounts themselves, can only be done properly if the underlying bookkeeping records are complete, accurate and up to date.

Like buildings, accounts will be dangerous if the foundations are not properly laid. Today's programme, therefore, is deep and varied. You will study several more aspects of bookkeeping and attempt two practical examples.

We will look at the following:

- the cash book
- the bank reconciliation
- other reconciliations and checks
- the journal
- petty cash
- the trial balance.

The cash book

Almost any set of accounting records involves the receiving and paying out of money. If there are only a few entries, it may all be recorded in the bank account and cash account in the nominal ledger. However, due to the number of entries, it is usual to maintain a separate cash book. Sometimes bank and cash are combined in one book and sometimes two books are kept. Today's work assumes that two books are kept.

Sometimes the cash book is really a posting medium to the appropriate nominal ledger account. In this respect it is rather like the day books studied yesterday. The cash book will have two sides, one for payments and one for receipts. The payments side would probably look like this.

Date	Cheque no.	Payee	Folio	Amount £
4 May	1234	Simpson and Co.	S3	200.68
9 May	1235	Jones Ltd	J8	33.11
14 May	–	Bank charges	39	10.00
17 May	1236	Wainrights	W1	111.00
19 May	1237	Cubitt Ltd	C9	44.00
				398.79

The total of £398.79 would be credited to the bank account in the nominal ledger.

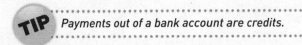

TIP *Payments out of a bank account are credits.*

Various accounts are debited and these are identified by the folio numbers.

In reality, there may be hundreds of entries. The posting may be made easier by analysing the payment amount over extra columns. For example, if there are three entries for bank charges, only the total of the bank charges need be posted, rather than three individual items.

The following is an example of a full cash book balanced at the month end.

Receipts Date		Folio	Amount £	Date			Folio	Payments Amount £
1 Sept.	Balance	b/d	800.00	1 Sept.	4001	Arkwright	PL3	29.16
4 Sept.	Cross and Co.	SL6	101.10	2 Sept.	4002	Rates	NL4	290.00
9 Sept.	Figg Ltd	SL12	17.11	6 Sept.	4003	Stevens Ltd	PL7	34.12
13 Sept.	Morgan Ltd	SL17	34.19	9 Sept.	4004	Wilson Bros	PL19	47.11
18 Sept.	Peters and Brown	SL3	700.00	12 Sept.	4005	Crabbe and Co.	PL8	39.12
30 Sept.	Trapp Ltd	SL22	1 091.00	17 Sept.	4006	Carter	PL2	200.00
				19 Sept.	4007	Jenkins	PL12	56.99
				23 Sept.	4008	Champion and Co	PL17	450.00
				24 Sept.	4009	Wages	NL4	290.00
				29 Sept.	4010	Barton and Hicks	PL1	300.00
				30 Sept.		Balance	c/d	1,006.90
			2,743.40					2,743.40
1 Oct.	Balance	b/d	1,006.90					

This is a completed cash book for the month of September. You will have noticed that the book has been ruled off and balanced, the first time this week that you have seen this done. The balancing may be done at any time but once a month is typical.

The balancing is done by adding the columns and writing in the difference on the side that has the smaller of the two figures. This is expressed as the balance carried down. The two columns then add to the same amount. The balancing figure is then transferred to the other column and becomes the opening balance in the next period.

In the example the balance brought down on 1 September is on the receipts side, which means that there is money in the bank and no overdraft. This is still the position when the account is balanced on 30 September.

The four-figure numbers before the names on the payments side are cheque numbers. This is optional and will assist when the bank reconciliation is done.

The bank reconciliation

It is good practice to write up the cash book frequently and to keep it up to date. That way, you will know what the statement balance will be when all items reach the bank. You will have prior knowledge if the account is close to an overdraft or an agreed limit.

Case study

The writer Ernest Hemingway often did not bother to bank cheques that he received, preferring instead to use them as bookmarks. After his death, his house was found to contain dozens of unbanked cheques, some as much as 20 years old. They were presented for payment and many of them were paid. This is an extreme example of one reason why the bank statement balance might not be the same as the cash book balance, and why it is necessary to reconcile the two balances.

Possible reasons for a difference in the two figures are as follows:

- Cheques written in the cash book have not yet been debited to the bank statement.
- Receipts written in the cash book have not yet been credited to the bank statement.
- Items have been debited to the bank statement that have not yet been written in the cash book. Common examples are direct debits, standing orders and bank charges.
- Receipts have been credited to the bank statement that have not yet been written in the cash book. This could, for example, be a credit transfer payment by a customer.
- You have made a mistake – perhaps the wrong amount has been written into the cash book or a paying-in slip has been added incorrectly.
- The bank has made a mistake. This is very unlikely, but it can happen.

Test your understanding

You should now be able to have a go at doing a bank reconciliation. The following is a simplified bank statement for the company whose cash book was given earlier in today's work. It is for September, corresponding with the period covered by the cash book. As it is a bank statement, receipts are printed on the right, the opposite side to the normal cash book layout.

Date	Detail	Payments £	Receipts £	Balance £
1 Sept.	Opening balance			800.00 cr
6 Sept.	Counter credit		101.10	
6 Sept.	4001	29.16		
6 Sept.	4002	290.00		581.94 cr
11 Sept.	Counter credit		17.11	599.05 cr
12 Sept.	Standing order – rates	105.16		493.89 cr
15 Sept.	Counter credit		34.19	
15 Sept.	4003	34.12		
15 Sept.	4004	47.11		
15 Sept.	Direct debit – water rates	61.82		385.03 cr
20 Sept.	Counter credit		700.00	
20 Sept.	Credit transfer received		349.21	1,434.24 cr
21 Sept.	4005	38.12		1,396.12 cr
30 Sept.	4008	450.00		946.12 cr

You must tick off the entries in the bank statement against those in the cash book and write out the differences. Do not worry about the best layout – just have a go and write it down. The answer is given at the end of today's work, but have a go before you check.

Other reconciliations and checks

If there is a bank account, you should periodically reconcile it with the cash book or with the appropriate account in the nominal ledger. You should also reconcile or check other accounts periodically. One of these is petty cash and this is considered shortly.

From time to time, you should check that all the sales ledger accounts add up to the sales ledger control account in the nominal ledger. Similarly, all the purchase ledger accounts should add up to the purchase ledger control account in the nominal ledger.

If you have any sort of suspense account, it is important that you analyse what items make up the balance.

A suspense account is, of course, an account where money is placed until a final accounting entry is decided.

I can reliably forecast that all sorts of nonsense will get dumped into the suspense account. I forecast this because it seems to happen to all suspense accounts. You must identify the items and take steps to clear them out. The list of potential reconciliations is a long one and it is good practice to reconcile where possible.

The journal

We have seen earlier this week that entries are made to the accounting records by means of the following **books of entry**:

- the sales day book
- the purchases day book
- the cash book.

Entries are also made by means of the returns inwards book, the returns outwards book and the petty cash book. The petty cash book is examined later today. The books of entry are completed by the journal, which is an important item in bookkeeping and worth explaining in some detail.

The journal is used to record important transactions that are not posted through the medium of any of the above books. You could just post the debits and credits to the right accounts without recording them in a book. Many bookkeepers do just this but it is much better to use a journal. This makes fraud and mistakes less likely, makes it easier to check the books, and, most importantly, gives you a narrative explanation for the entries. Auditors favour the use of a journal.

The journal is ruled to show the date, a reference number for the entry, the identity and amount of the account to be credited, the identity and amount of the account to be debited, and a narrative explanation. An example of a journal entry is as follows:

		Debit	Credit
1 March	Bad debts written off	£1,000.00	
JV99	Curzon & Co		£1,000.00

Petty cash

The word 'petty' means small or trivial, and the purpose of the petty cash system is to allow small and trivial disbursements to be made. This limitation may not always be apparent to colleagues who will try to obtain large sums of money from it. Nevertheless, the purpose is to handle small sums of money.

A typical petty cash book is very wide, has two sides, and has a considerable number of columns for analysis. This makes it difficult to reproduce here, but the following is a simplified example of how the payments side typically looks.

Date	Details of expense	Voucher no.	Total £	Stamps £	Petrol £
2 May	Stamps	1	10.00	10.00	
16 May	Petrol	2	18.48		18.48
29 May	Stamps	3	10.00	10.00	
			38.48	20.00	18.48
May	Balance c/d		11.52		
			50.00		

In practice, there would, of course, be many more entries and a further dozen or so analysis columns to record the different categories of expense (milk, stationery, etc.).

Note that the total column is always used and this is the total amount paid out on each voucher. If someone is claiming £10 for stamps and £10 for petrol, £20 would be entered in the total column.

The imprest system

The example above assumes that the imprest system is in use and that the float is £50. The imprest system is loved by auditors and is much superior to other systems.

Under the imprest system the amount of money in the petty cash box, plus the payments made and recorded in the book, should add up to the amount of the float. If they do not, a mistake has been made. In the previous example a cheque for £38.48 would be written and cashed. This would restore the float to £50, which would then be the opening balance for June.

The accounting entries to record the May transactions would be:

Postage account   £20.00 debit
Petrol account   £18.48 debit
Petty cash account   £38.48 credit

The entry for the reimbursement cheque would be:

Petty cash account   £38.48 debit
Bank account   £38.48 credit

After all the entries have been posted, the petty cash account should have a balance of £50 debit in the nominal ledger. It is an asset account and there is £50 cash to support it. A £50 cheque would have been written on Day 1.

The trial balance

The trial balance is not an account and it does not involve posting. It is the listing of all the balances in the ledger.

There are two very good reasons for taking out a trial balance:

1 It is one of the steps towards preparing the profit and loss account and the balance sheet.
2 It is proof that, subject to certain exceptions described below, the books are in order.

It is good practice to take out a trial balance regularly, perhaps once a month. This means that, if there is a mistake to be found, only a month's entries need be checked. Of course, in a computerized bookkeeping system it should be guaranteed that the system balances and that the total of the debit balances equals the total of the credit balances.

Taking out a trial balance

You will remember that for every debit there must be a credit. It follows that the total of all the debit balances must equal the total of all the credit balances. If they do not do so, then a mistake has been made. Taking out a trial balance will find this out.

There are limitations to the proofs provided by a trial balance. It may balance and yet not disclose the following two types of error:

- a compensating error: this is two mistakes for the same amount, one increasing or reducing the debits and one increasing or reducing the credits
- the right amount posted to the wrong account.

Both these types of error are nasty and you may never realize that a mistake has been made. They each mean that two accounts are wrong.

A difference on the trial balance will disclose one of the following mistakes:

- a wrong addition on an account
- a mistake in writing out the brought forward balances
- one side of an entry not posted (double entry not complete)
- posting of wrong amount
- a missing ledger sheet.

How to conduct a trial balance

You might find the cause of a trial balance difference by means of a random search. However, it is much better to conduct the search in a systematic manner. You *must* locate the cause of the difference if you do the following in a *systematic* way:

1 Check the listing of the balances within the trial balance.
2 Check the addition of the trial balance.
3 Check the listing of the opening balances. These are either the balances brought down or the balances at the time that the last trial balance was agreed.
4 Check the addition of each individual account within the trial balance. Check from the brought forward balances or the balances making up the last trial balance.
5 Tick each individual posting during the period under review. Every debit should have a matching credit and there should be no unticked entries at the end.

If done properly, this must find the difference.

Test your understanding

We will finish today with a simple example of a trial balance, a series of postings and the new trial balance. The new trial balance is given at the end of today's work, but prepare it for yourself before checking the answer.

Summarized trial balance

	Debit £	Credit £
Capital account		50,000
Sales account		1,000,000
Sales ledger creditors		20,000
Cost of sales account	500,000	
Stock account	300,000	
Overhead account	190,000	
Bank account	80,000	
	1,070,000	1,070,000

Cash sales of £400,000 are made. Cost of sales is 50% of sales. £300,000 is spent on overheads, half on credit and half for cash. £600,000 fixed assets are purchased for cash.

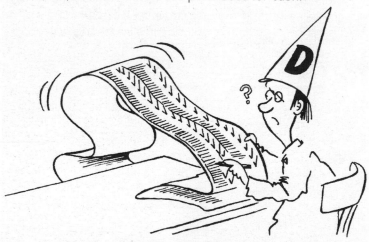

Summary

Today we examined several more essential aspects of bookkeeping. We have:

- studied the layout and operation of the cash book and the postings from it
- studied bank reconciliations and attempted an example
- considered other reconciliations and checks
- examined the journal
- considered petty cash, especially the imprest system
- examined trial balances and tried working from one trial balance through to another.

Tomorrow we will look at how to prepare for the accounts.

SUNDAY
MONDAY
TUESDAY
WEDNESDAY
THURSDAY
FRIDAY
SATURDAY

Test your understanding
Answers

Bank reconciliation

Cash book balance at 30 September		1,006.90 dr
Add cheques not yet presented:		
4006	200.00	
4007	56.99	
4009	290.00	
4010	300.00	
		846.99
		1,853.89
Add credit on statement not in cash book		349.21
		2,203.10
Less receipt in cash book not on statement		1,091.00
		1,112.10
Less payments on statement not in cash book		
Standing order – rates	105.16	
Direct debit – water rates	61.82	
		166.98
		945.12
Add difference to be investigated (cheque 4005 for £39.12 entered by bank as £38.12)		1.00
As per bank statement balance at 30 September		946.12 dr

This is not easy, so congratulations if you got it right. It does illustrate all the principles effectively.

Trial balance

	Debit £	Credit £
Capital account		50,000
Sales account		1,400,000
Sales ledger creditors		170,000
Cost of sales account	700,000	
Stock account	100,000	
Overhead account	490,000	
Bank account		270,000
Fixed asset accounts	600,000	
	1,890,000	1,890,000

Fact-check (answers at the back)

1. What should happen to the total of the payments recorded in the cash book?
   a) It should be debited to bank account in the nominal ledger ❑
   b) It should be credited to bank account in the nominal ledger ❑
   c) It should be added to the accumulated total of payments made in previous periods ❑
   d) Nothing ❑

2. What happens to the total of payments for stationery recorded in the cash book?
   a) It should be debited to stationery account in the nominal ledger ❑
   b) It should be credited to stationery account in the nominal ledger ❑
   c) It should be added to the accumulated total of payments made for stationery in previous periods ❑
   d) Nothing ❑

3. What happens to the closing balance when the cash book is ruled off at the end of a period?
   a) It is entered on the same side as the opening balance in the next period ❑
   b) It is entered on the opposite side as the opening balance in the next period ❑
   c) It is posted to the bank account in the nominal ledger ❑
   d) Nothing ❑

4. What is the journal used for?
   a) To keep a record of important events ❑
   b) To reconcile different ledgers ❑
   c) To reconcile different accounts ❑
   d) To record important transactions that are not posted through the medium of the other books ❑

5. Which of the following are advantages of using a journal rather than posting directly to the nominal ledger?
   a) Fraud and mistakes are less likely ❑
   b) The narrative explanation may be useful ❑
   c) Auditors like it ❑
   d) All of the above ❑

6. An employee is reimbursed in cash £10 for the purchase of biscuits. In which book will the entry be made?
   a) The cash book ❑
   b) The journal ❑
   c) The petty cash book ❑
   d) The purchases day book ❑

7. Which of the following is a feature of the imprest system for petty cash?
   a) It is impressive ❑
   b) There is a float of a fixed amount ❑
   c) It is not possible to run out of money ❑
   d) Employees will not claim unreasonably large sums ❑

8. What is a trial balance?
a) A listing of all the balances in the ledger ❏
b) A particular type of account ❏
c) Another name for the profit and loss account ❏
d) Another name for the balance sheet ❏

9. Which of the following mistakes will *not* be disclosed by a trial balance?
a) One side of an entry not posted (double entry not complete) ❏
b) A mistake in writing out the brought forward balances ❏
c) The right amount posted to the wrong account ❏
d) Posting of wrong amount ❏

10. What is a compensating error?
a) Posting of wrong amount ❏
b) A wrong addition on the account ❏
c) A mistake in listing or adding the trial balance ❏
d) Two mistakes for the same amount, one increasing or reducing the debits and one increasing or reducing the credits ❏

WEDNESDAY

Preparation for the accounts

Now that we have learned the basic principles of bookkeeping and discovered how to prepare accurate and complete bookkeeping records, we can turn our attention to the process involved in preparing the final accounts. However, there is more work to be done first.

Today we must look at important accounting entries which are not yet recorded in the trial balance but which are vital to the preparation of accurate accounts. We then conclude today's work by seeing how the trial balance is adjusted to reflect these entries.

The programme is:

- accruals
- prepayments
- reserves and provisions
- depreciation
- posting final adjustments and the extended trial balance.

Accruals

We concluded yesterday's work by considering the trial balance. This should accurately reflect the position after posting all the entries. But what about charges that have not yet been put into the accounts? Sometimes a supplier may be late submitting an invoice. If you work in a large accounts office, you will know that an occasional invoice may be submitted a year or more after the event.

Furthermore, suppliers' invoices may be lost or held up pending approval. The more quickly the books are closed off after the end of the accounting period, the more numerous will be the invoices not entered.

These problems can be overcome by entering what are called accruals. Accruals are **costs incurred but not yet entered**. They are calculated in one of two ways:

1 a specific invoice received after the close off
   – If the electricity bill to 31 March is £1,507.46 and accounts are done for the year to 31 March, then you will accrue either £1,507 or £1,500.
2 an informed estimate
   – If the electricity bill averages £1,000 a quarter and the last bill is up to 15 March, it would be reasonable to accrue £170 at 31 March. It is usual for most accruals to be informed estimates.

The accounting entry is to debit the account of the expense (e.g. electricity) and to credit the accruals account. The accruals account is a liability account because it is money owing by the business.

Prepayments

A prepayment is the exact opposite of an accrual, which is a cost incurred but not yet entered. A prepayment is **a cost entered but not yet incurred**.

A prepayment may be necessary because a supplier has raised an invoice early, or because you have left the books open to catch as many invoices as possible and one from the next period has slipped through. For example, an invoice dated 3 July may slip through if you make the accounts up to 30 June but leave the books open for two weeks beyond that date.

More usually, a prepayment may be necessary because an invoice has been entered that covers a benefit to be received in the future. A common example is insurance, which may be paid a year in advance.

Prepayments in practice

Consider an insurance invoice for £12,000 that has been paid on 31 December for insurance cover over the following 12 months. Let us assume that the business prepared its accounts at 30 June. Obviously, unless an adjustment is made, overheads will be too large and the profit will be too small.

The answer is to prepay six-twelfths of £12,000, which equals £6,000. Insurance (an overhead account) is credited with £6,000 and the prepayments account is debited £6,000.

The prepayments account is an asset account because it is money paid in advance for goods and services. It is like the deposit that you may pay in February for your summer holiday to be taken in August.

You may be asking what eventually happens to the entries for accruals and prepayments after the accounts have been prepared. The answer is that they are reversed. This is explained later today.

Test your understanding

You should now take a few moments to test your understanding by writing down the entries for the following. The answers are given at the end of today.

A staff restaurant prepares accounts at 31 May

- A £70 invoice for bread from the wholesalers dated 8 June has been entered into the books.
- The telephone account for the quarter to 31 March was £600. No later invoice has been received.
- Six months' water rates in advance totalling £900 were paid on 31 March.
- Food with a total value of £700 was delivered to the canteen on 29 May. No invoice has been received.
- Wages average £350 a week and are paid weekly in arrears. Payment has been made for work done up to 26 May. (A seven-day week is worked.)

Reserves

On Monday you read that reserves were part of the capital of a business and represented money belonging to the shareholders or other owners. However, the term has a very different meaning as well.

Reserves are made to cover an event that may well happen (or has actually happened) but which is not adequately recorded in the books.

Bad debt reserves

A bad debt reserve is an easily understood example. Company A made a credit sale of £100,000 to Company B. The entries in the books of Company A were:

- Sales account   £100,000 credit
- Trade debtors' account   £100,000 debit

Good news so far. The balance of the sales account will eventually be credited to the profit and loss account and will increase profit. It is expected that Company B will soon send a cheque for £100,000 to clear the trade debtors' account. But Company B's chairman is arrested and charged with fraud, the directors resign, the company goes into liquidation, and the liquidator forecasts an eventual dividend of 10p in the pound to unsecured creditors.

To put it mildly, the books of Company A do not reflect the true position. They overstate the true profit by £90,000. Company A will need the following entry in its books:

- Bad debt reserve account   £90,000 credit
- Bad debt account   £90,000 debit

The bad debts account is a charge to the profit and loss account. This reduces the £100,000 sale contribution to a realistic £10,000.

The bad debt reserve account is placed against the trade debtors' account in the balance sheet. It is thus reduced to £10,000, which is the amount expected to be paid eventually.

Bad debt reserves may be against specific debts as above, or they may be a realistic general reserve. For example, a book club sells books to the public by post and sends out the books before payment is made. At any one time it is owed money by many thousands of different customers. Each debt is individually small. Experience may show that a bad debt reserve of, say, 5% of the total outstanding is necessary.

Provisions

Provisions are very similar to reserves and, in practice, the two terms are almost interchangeable. Reserves and provisions are necessary for more than just bad debts. The list is very long and you may well be able to think of some circumstances that relate to a business with which you are familiar. The following are just some of the possibilities.

● Provision for settlement discounts payable

Suppose that your business offers 5% settlement discount to all customers who pay within 30 days of invoice date. Unless you make a provision, you will overstate the profits. Not all customers will take advantage of the settlement discount so perhaps a provision of 4% of the total sum outstanding would be realistic.

● Provision for fulfilling warranty claim obligations

Suppose that you supply double-glazed windows and guarantee to repair faulty workmanship free of charge for up to ten years after installation. A realistic provision for the cost of future repairs would be necessary.

● Provision for settlement of outstanding legal claims

These could be for alleged negligence, faulty workmanship, wrongful dismissal, libel or many other matters. Again, a realistic estimate of the eventual cost should be provided.

● Provision for losses on a contract or joint venture

Perhaps one of these has gone wrong. Your organization has a legal obligation to complete the work, but it is clear that a loss will be made at the end. Provision should be made for the loss as soon as it can realistically be foreseen. You should not wait to charge the profit and loss account in future years.

In all cases the accounting entry is:

- Credit a suitably named reserve or provision account
- Debit the appropriate account in the profit and loss section.

Depreciation

Current assets are assets with a value available to the business in the short term, usually taken to mean up to a year. Examples are cash, stock, and trade debtors (money owing by customers).

Fixed assets are assets with a value available in the long term, usually taken to mean more than a year. Examples are motor vehicles, leases, plant and machinery, and computer equipment.

Some fixed assets hold their value indefinitely, but most do not. The value of most fixed assets diminishes either with time (e.g. leases), with wear and tear (e.g. plant and equipment), or with both (e.g. cars). Computer equipment frequently diminishes in value due to obsolescence.

Depreciation in action

Perhaps the simplest example of a depreciating fixed asset is a lease. Take leasehold property purchased for £300,000, and with ten years of the lease remaining. On the day that the property is purchased it is worth £300,000. Ten years later it is worth nothing. Its value falls by £30,000 each year. If the accounts do not recognize this, both the profit and the value of the assets will be overstated.

It is therefore necessary to write off most fixed assets over a period of time. A formula must be found that fairly reflects the reduction in value. In the case of the £300,000 lease described in the example the annual bookkeeping entry is:

- depreciation account   £30,000 debit
- leasehold property account   £30,000 credit.

The depreciation account is a profit and loss account item and it reduces the profit. The credit to the leasehold property account reduces the value of the asset, which you will remember is a debit balance. This is the straight-line method of depreciation, which is the most common and the simplest. It involves writing off an equal amount over a fixed number of years.

Another common method is the reducing balance method. This writes off a given percentage of the remaining balance. A feature of this method is that the value of the asset in the books can never quite reach zero. This is usually realistic; after all, even a 20-year-old car is worth something.

An example of this is an item of machinery purchased for £100,000 and written off at 25% per year on the reducing balance method. The depreciation charge will be as follows:

- **Year 1**   25% × £100,000 = £25,000
- **Year 2**   25% × £75,000 = £18,750
- **Year 3**   25% × £56,250 = £14,063

There are other methods as well. Care must be taken to choose an appropriate depreciation policy and it must be applied consistently from year to year.

Posting final adjustments and the extended trial balance

Yesterday we saw that the production of the trial balance is a key stage in preparing accounts. We finish today's work by considering how the trial balance is finalized for the preparation of the accounts.

If the accounts are very simple and everything is up to date, there may not be any further entries to post. In these cases the accountant can proceed directly to prepare the accounts. We will look at accounts preparation in detail on Thursday and Friday.

This is unusual, though, especially if there are a lot of entries. It is usually necessary to list the trial balance, open the accounts for the next period and then work through a list of adjustments to the trial balance. There are nearly always accruals and prepayments. There are often reserves and provisions to enter and mistakes to be corrected, and there may be many other adjustments as well.

There are two basic approaches for posting the adjustments – actually posting the entries or making an extended trial balance – and we will consider these in turn. It is likely that a computerized system will handle the posting of the final adjustments, but the following explains the principles.

Posting the entries

All the adjustments are posted in the ledgers and then a new trial balance is listed. This new trial balance is used to prepare the accounts. All the adjustment entries are then reverse posted into the ledgers in the next period. This reverse posting is necessary because the ledgers have to be restored to the position before the adjustments.

This may be difficult to understand, but consider an accrual of £1,000 for a late telephone bill. The accrual is a debit to the overhead account. In the next period the reverse posting puts a credit of £1,000 into the overhead account. When the actual invoice for £1,000 arrives, it is a debit and cancels out the credit, leaving a nil balance. This is correct because it was a late invoice that should affect profit only in the earlier period.

Computerized accounting systems usually operate in this way. This is because it is relatively simple for the computer to be programmed to reverse post automatically into the following period.

The extended trial balance

The second approach is to list all the adjustments into extra columns to the trial balance (one debit column and one credit column). The trial balance is then repeated, taking account of the adjustments. The whole thing is contained in one page and there are six columns in total (sometimes eight columns but we will not bother with this). It is extremely important that all the adjustments are properly cross-referenced to a full list of the changes and a narrative explanation of them.

Test your understanding

We will conclude today by looking at an extended trial balance for Bridget Murphy, a public relations consultant. She commences business on 1 July and the extended trial balance is at the end of her first year in business on the following 30 June. Note that the title and date should be given at the top.

The extended trial balance is given below and you should study it carefully. It incorporates adjustments to reflect the following:

- Motor vehicle and office equipment should both be depreciated by 25%.
- Bridget has not yet entered an invoice for £5,000 for work that she has done.
- Bank interest to 30 June not yet entered into the books is £2,643.
- On 21 May Bridget paid £2,400 insurance to cover a year in advance.
- Bridget has received invoices as follows but not entered them into the books:
  - Office expenses   £1,800
  - Travel expenses   £246
  - Stationery   £679.
- Her telephone account averages £1,800 a quarter and she has paid the bill up to 31 May.
- Bridget believes that £1,000 owing to her will turn out to be a bad debt.

	Opening Trial Balance		Adjustments		Closing Trial Balance	
	Debit £	Credit £	Debit £	Credit £	Debit £	Credit £
Motor vehicles	20,000.00				20,000.00	
Office equipment	15,000.00				15,000.00	
Depreciation of motor vehicles				5,000.00		5,000.00
Depreciation of office equipment				3,750.00		3,750.00
Bank account		23,185.16				23,185.16
Trade debtors	5,708.31		5,000.00		10,708.31	
Trade creditors		661.19				661.19
Reserve for bad debts				1,000.00		1,000.00
Accruals				5,968.00		5,968.00
Prepayments			2,400.00		2,400.00	
Fees invoiced		62,000.00		5,000.00		67,000.00
Salaries	12,000.00				12,000.00	
Insurance	4,600.00			2,400.00	2,200.00	
Office expenses	7,309.14		1,800.00		9,109.14	
Travel expenses	11,111.18		246.00		11,357.18	
Stationery	3,209.47		679.00		3,888.47	
Telephone	6,908.25		600.00		7,508.25	
Interest			2,643.00		2,643.00	
Bad debts			1,000.00		1,000.00	
Depreciation			8,750.00		8,750.00	
	85,846.35	85,846.35	23,118.00	23,118.00	106,564.35	106,564.35

Summary

Today we have examined some of the calculations that have to be made before the final accounts are prepared, and we have seen how these are incorporated into the trial balance. Specifically we have:

- studied accruals and prepayments
- tested our understanding of accruals and prepayments
- studied reserves and provisions
- studied depreciation
- seen how the adjustments are entered into the accounts
- studied the extended trial balance.

Tomorrow we move on to a detailed examination of the profit and loss account.

SUNDAY
MONDAY
TUESDAY
WEDNESDAY
THURSDAY
FRIDAY
SATURDAY

Test your understanding

Answers

A staff restaurant prepares accounts at 31 May

	Debit £	Credit £
	70	
Food purchased account		70
Accruals account		400
Telephone account	400	
Prepayments account	600	
Water rates account		600
Accruals account		700
Food purchased account	700	
Accruals account		250
Wages account	250	

Fact-check (answers at the back)

1. What is an accrual?
   a) A cost entered but not yet incurred ☐
   b) A cost incurred but not yet entered ☐
   c) Total costs for the period ☐
   d) Cheques issued but not yet recorded on the bank statement ☐

2. If a telephone bill is normally about £3,000 per quarter and the last bill received was for the quarter to 30 September, what should be the accrual in the accounts for the year to 30 November?
   a) £1,000 ☐
   b) £2,000 ☐
   c) £3,000 ☐
   d) £12,000 ☐

3. What is a prepayment?
   a) A cost entered but not yet incurred ☐
   b) A cost incurred but not yet entered ☐
   c) Total costs for the period ☐
   d) Cheques issued but not yet recorded on the bank statement ☐

4. A supplier submits an invoice for £12,000 dated 1 October for a year's rent in advance for the period commencing 1 November. It is entered in the books for the period to 30 September. What should be the prepayment in the accounts for the year to 30 September?
   a) £13,000 ☐
   b) £1,000 ☐
   c) £12,000 ☐
   d) £6,000 ☐

5. A company is owed £10,000,000 by its customers. It offers a prompt payment discount of 3% and experience shows that about two-thirds of the customers take advantage of it. What sum should be created as a reserve?
   a) £100,000 ☐
   b) £150,000 ☐
   c) £200,000 ☐
   d) £300,000 ☐

6. A company has created a bad debt reserve of £6,000 in respect of money owing by Company X. However, Company X subsequently pays £1,500. What entry must be made in the bad debt reserve account?
   a) £6,000 debit ☐
   b) £4,500 debit ☐
   c) £4,500 credit ☐
   d) £1,500 debit ☐

7. A car costing £60,000 is written off at 25% per year using the straight-line method. What is the depreciation charge in the third year?
   a) £60,000 ❏
   b) £45,000 ❏
   c) £30,000 ❏
   d) £15,000 ❏

8. A car costing £60,000 is written off at 25% per year using the reducing balance method. What is the depreciation charge in the third year?
   a) £15,000 ❏
   b) £11,250 ❏
   c) £8,437 ❏
   d) £6,328 ❏

9. Given the facts in Question 8, when will the car be written down to nil value?
   a) After four years ❏
   b) After six years ❏
   c) After eight years ❏
   d) Never ❏

10. On 1 July a company purchases leasehold property for £500,000. The lease has 20 years left to run. What should be the depreciation charge in the year to 31 December?
    a) £12,500 ❏
    b) £25,000 ❏
    c) £50,000 ❏
    d) £500,000 ❏

SUNDAY

MONDAY

TUESDAY

WEDNESDAY

THURSDAY

FRIDAY

SATURDAY

THURSDAY

The profit and
loss account

During the first four days of this week we have worked through the principles of bookkeeping up to the extended trial balance. We are now ready to see the accounts resulting from this work. Today we will look at the internal profit and loss account that is produced for the benefit of managers, and tomorrow we will study the other main part of the accounts, the balance sheet. On Saturday you will learn how to put together published accounts.

Once again, the steps are explained in detail to help your understanding, even though in most offices computers will of course do much of the work. Today you will learn exactly what a profit and loss account is, and how it works. Although, as Benjamin Franklin said, only two things are certain in life: death and taxes, we will not be discussing taxation in accounts until Friday's chapter.

The programme today also covers examples of:

- a straightforward profit and loss account
- a trading business
- a manufacturing business.

We will also look at two further important points about profit and loss accounts.

What is the profit and loss account?

The profit and loss account is a **summary of all the revenue and expense items** occurring in a specified period of time. The profit and loss account should be properly headed and the period of time stated.

The period is usually a year, especially in the case of published accounts, but you may encounter other periods. Internal profit statements prepared for management may be done weekly, monthly, quarterly or for some other convenient period. The selection of the period does matter. Consider a typical greetings card shop preparing a profit statement for the six months to 31 August. Twenty-five per cent of a year's turnover comes in the five weeks ending on 24 December.

The bookkeeping procedure is as follows.

1 Make sure that everything is posted up to date.
2 Post all the final adjustments. This was explained yesterday.
3 List the final adjusted trial balance, although a computerized system will probably make this unnecessary.
4 Extract the revenue and expense accounts and list these separately. If the credit balances exceed the debit balances, there is a profit. If the debit balances are greater, there is a loss.

5 Open the ledger for the next period. All the revenue and expense accounts will be opened with a nil balance. The net profit or net loss will be transferred to the capital account, thus increasing or decreasing the amount of capital that the proprietor has invested in the business. This ensures that the trial balance continues to balance.

6 The accruals and prepayments are reverse posted into the new period.

A straightforward profit and loss account

There are more things to learn when goods are purchased for resale and stocks are held. A step beyond that is when manufacturing takes place. We will study all this later today, but first of all you need to understand a straightforward profit and loss account. The examples are well illustrated with the figures for Bridget Murphy, the public relations consultant whose extended trial balance was listed yesterday.

Please refer back to that extended trial balance. You should be able to recognize which accounts are revenue and expense accounts. You should therefore be able to follow how her profit and loss account is extracted. It is given below.

Bridget Murphy	Profit and loss account for year to 30 June	
	£	£
Fees invoiced		67,000
Less expenses:		
Salaries	12,000	
Insurance	2,200	
Office expenses	9,109	
Travel expenses	11,357	
Stationery	3,888	
Telephone	7,508	
Interest	2,643	
Bad debts	1,000	
Depreciation	8,750	
		58,455
Net Profit		8,545

Test your understanding

Now test your knowledge of the profit and loss account by preparing one yourself, using the following example. The answer is given at the end of today's work, but prepare the account before looking at it.

Bernard Smith starts work as a painter and decorator on 1 June

He does not hold stocks of materials as he buys just enough for each job. At the following 31 May his trial balance is as follows:

	Debit	Credit
	£	£
Motor van	6,000.00	
Ladder and tools	1,000.00	
Bank account	300.00	
Trade debtors	700.00	
Trade creditors		400.00
Invoiced sales		15,000.00
Materials used	2,000.00	
Motor expenses	1,400.00	
Other overhead costs	4,000.00	
	15,400.00	15,400.00

Bernard is advised that he should depreciate the motor van by 25%, and the ladder and tools by 10%.

He believes that half the trade debtors are an irrecoverable bad debt. He holds an invoice for materials for £600 and an overheads invoice for £200. Neither has been entered into the books. He has paid £500 for a year's insurance in advance.

A customer has complained about bad workmanship. Bernard has agreed to spend £200 on putting it right.

A trading business

So far we have only considered businesses that do not hold stock. It is now time to see how the accounts deal with this problem.

You will, I hope, quickly see that the profit and loss account must only show the cost of the goods sold in the period. You will obtain a wrong figure, perhaps a ridiculous figure, if the cost of goods purchased in the period is used.

The cost of goods sold in the period is obtained in the following way:

1 Take the value of stock at the beginning of the period.
2 Add purchases during the period.
3 Subtract the value of stock at the end of the period.

The value of stock at the beginning and end of the period may be established by stocktaking. If financial controls are extremely good, they may be calculated figures, with occasional stock checks to prove the system and the figures. If there has been any theft or other form of stock shrinkage, stock will be reduced and consequently the cost of sales will be increased.

The principle is illustrated by the following profit and loss account of a school tuck shop. In this simple example there are no costs other than the cost of the food sold.

- Sales in the month of February total £430.
- Stock at 31 January was £100.
- Stock at 28 February was £120.
- Purchases in February were £380.

School tuck shop
Profit and loss account for February month

	£	£
Sales		430
Stock at 31 January	100	
Add purchases in February	<u>380</u>	
	480	
Less stock at 28 February	<u>120</u>	
		<u>360</u>
Net profit		<u>70</u>

Exactly the same principles apply in the profit and loss accounts of big stores and supermarkets – although, of course, the figures are considerably bigger! These companies buy food and other products from their suppliers, they have stock checks at the beginning and end of each trading period (or they calculate the stock) and they sell to the public.

A manufacturing business

You have already seen that the profit and loss account of a trading company must contain only the costs of the goods actually sold. The cost of goods purchased and held in stock must be excluded. For the same reason the profit and loss account of a manufacturing company must contain only the manufacturing costs of the goods actually sold in the period. The manufacturing costs of goods not sold must be excluded.

As with a trading company, it will probably be necessary for a manufacturing business to stocktake at the beginning and end of the period, but if controls are very good it may not always be necessary.

Sometimes the manufacturing costs are shown in a separate manufacturing account. This leads to a manufacturing profit that is carried forward to the profit and loss account. Other costs are deducted in the main profit and loss account to give the overall profit or loss. Similarly, trading activities are sometimes shown in a separate trading account. This method of presentation is optional and not followed here. We will show everything in the main profit and loss account.

These are the key points to remember:

- There are definite starting and finishing dates.
- Total sales appear at the top.
- The net profit or loss is at the bottom.
- All revenue and expense accounts are included.
- Only expenditure on goods actually sold is included.

The following example shows the principles for a manufacturing business.

Bognor Cases Ltd manufactures and sells suitcases

- Sales in the year to 30 June 2015 were £1,000,000.
- Purchases of raw materials and components in the year totalled £400,000.
- Stock at 30 June 2014 was £320,000 and at 30 June 2015 it was £365,000.
- Wages of production staff were £216,000.
- Factory rent was £110,000 and power costs were £40,000.

- Other production costs were £40,000.
- Salaries totalled £82,000. Other overheads were £66,000.

Bognor Cases Ltd
Profit and loss account for year to 30 June 2015

	£	£
Sales		1,000,000
Stock at 30.6.14	320,000	
Add purchases	400,000	
	720,000	
Less stock at 30.6.15	365,000	
	355,000	
Production wages	216,000	
Factory rent	110,000	
Power costs	40,000	
Other production costs	40,000	
Cost of manufacturing		761,000
		239,000
Less overheads		
Salaries	82,000	
Other overheads	66,000	
		148,000
Net profit		91,000

Note that the costs are split into two sections. All costs relating to the product and manufacturing go into the top part. These contribute to the cost of manufacturing and to the subtotal, which is the manufacturing profit. Overhead costs go below this subtotal.

Test your understanding

You should find the following exercise quite easy. The answer is given at the end of today's work, but set it out before looking.

North West Garden Novelties Ltd manufactures and sells garden gnomes

- Sales in the year to 30 April 2015 were £600,000.

- Purchases of materials totalled £200,000. Stock at 30 April 2014 was £50,000 and stock at 30 April 2015 was £40,000.
- Production wages in the year were £280,000 and other production costs were £90,000. Total overheads were £60,000.

Two key concepts

To complete today's study of the profit and loss account, we will consider two further important concepts.

Match cost to income

When we studied trading companies and manufacturing companies, we saw that the costs of goods sold, and not of any other goods, should be brought into the account.

The same applies to all the costs, and an example of where it is particularly relevant is a long-term construction contract, such as building London's Olympic Stadium. When 30% of a project is included in income, it is vital that costs exactly relating to this 30% are included.

Prepare accounts on a prudent basis

Again, construction projects are a good example. Profits should not be taken before they have been earned. A loss should be taken when it can be realistically foreseen, but a profit should only be taken after it has been earned.

Summary

This Thursday we have learned about the profit and loss account, the summary of all the revenue and expense items in a business that occur over a specified period of time. We have also tested our understanding with some practical exercises. We should now have:

- understood exactly what a profit and loss account is
- studied a simple example
- looked at trading businesses
- looked at manufacturing businesses
- briefly looked at two important concepts.

Tomorrow we progress to the other main part of the accounts, the balance sheet.

Test your understanding

Answers

Bernard Smith

Bernard Smith
Profit and loss account for year to 31 May

	£	£
Invoiced sales		15,000
Less costs:		
Materials used	2,200	
Motor expenses	1,400	
Other overhead costs	3,700	
Depreciation	1,600	
Bad debt	350	
Remedial work	200	
		9,450
Net profit		**5,550**

North West Garden Novelties

North West Novelties Ltd
Profit and loss account for year to 30 April 2015

	£	£
Sales		600,000
Stock at 30.4.14	50,000	
Add purchases	200,000	
	250,000	
Less stock at 30.4.15	40,000	
	210,000	
Production wages	280,000	
Other production costs	90,000	
Cost of manufacturing		580,000
		20,000
Less total overheads		60,000
Net loss for year		**(40,000)**

This is the first time today that we have encountered a loss.
Note that it is shown by means of a bracketed figure.

Fact-check (answers at the back)

1. Where do the figures in the profit and loss account come from?
   a) The balance sheet ❑
   b) The cash book ❑
   c) The trial balance ❑
   d) The sales ledger and the purchase ledger ❑

2. What happens to the net profit or loss?
   a) It stays where it is ❑
   b) It is transferred to the capital account ❑
   c) It is paid out as a dividend (if it is a profit) ❑
   d) It is invested ❑

3. Which accounts go into the profit and loss account?
   a) The revenue and expense accounts ❑
   b) The asset and liability accounts ❑
   c) The capital accounts ❑
   d) All of them ❑

4. What must happen in the profit and loss account if the business buys and sells goods?
   a) The cost of goods purchased in the period must be included ❑
   b) Stock at the beginning of the period must be included ❑
   c) Stock at the end of the period must be included ❑
   d) The cost of goods sold in the period must be included ❑

5. How do you ascertain the cost of goods sold in the period?
   a) Closing stock plus purchases less opening stock ❑
   b) Opening stock plus purchases less closing stock ❑
   c) An informed estimate by a trained person ❑
   d) Opening stock less closing stock ❑

6. What is the effect in the profit and loss account of the theft of stock?
   a) Stock is reduced ❑
   b) Overheads are increased ❑
   c) Sales are reduced ❑
   d) The cost of sales is increased ❑

7. Where does factory rent appear in the profit and loss account of a manufacturing company?
   a) In the overheads ❑
   b) In the cost of manufacturing ❑
   c) Added to the purchases of materials and components ❑
   d) As a deduction from net profit ❑

8. It is expected that a long-term project will make a loss. When should the loss be brought into the profit and loss account?
   a) In equal instalments over the life of the project ❑
   b) On completion of the project ❑
   c) As soon as it can realistically be foreseen ❑
   d) One year after completion of the project ❑

9. Where do assets appear in the profit and loss account?
a) As part of sales ☐
b) As a reduction in overheads ☐
c) As an addition to the net profit ☐
d) Assets do not appear in the profit and loss account ☐

10. Which of the following statements about the profit and loss account is true?
a) It covers the period of time stated in the heading ☐
b) It is at the fixed date stated in the heading ☐
c) It must cover a period of a year ☐
d) It must cover a period of at least a month ☐

FRIDAY

The balance sheet

The two main constituent parts of a set of accounts are the profit and loss account and the balance sheet. Now that you are familiar with the principles of the profit and loss account, studied yesterday, we can progress to the balance sheet. Today you will learn exactly what a balance sheet is, and the programme also covers:

- the concept of ownership (the capital accounts)
- the layout of the balance sheet
- how to prepare your own balance sheet
- the main balance sheet headings: fixed assets, current assets, current liabilities, net current assets and long-term liabilities.

These are the concepts you will need to know about before you can gain a full understanding of published accounts.

What is a balance sheet?

You can help yourself remember the answer to this question by thinking of the literal meaning of the two words 'balance' and 'sheet'.

Balance This means that the balance sheet must balance. There are two sides to it and they must total to the same figure. Put another way, the sum of the debit balances must equal the sum of the credit balances; all the figures come from the extended trial balance.

Sheet This means literally a sheet of paper on which the figures are listed.

Earlier in the week we saw that there are five different types of account. Yesterday we saw that the revenue and expense accounts are extracted from the extended trial balance and that these accounts make up the profit and loss account. The balance sheet is made up from everything that is left. These are the three remaining types of account:

- asset accounts (debit balances)
- liability accounts (credit balances)
- capital accounts (normally credit balances)

The profit or loss at the bottom of the profit and loss account is added to, or subtracted from, the capital accounts. The result is that the balance sheet balances, which is essential. We saw yesterday that the profit and loss account covers a given period of time. If trading is continuing, the profit or loss would be different if the period were to be one day shorter or longer. The balance sheet is not like that. It is a listing of the balances on just one fixed date, almost always the date at the end of the trading period.

The concept of ownership

Asset and liability accounts are relatively easy to comprehend, but you may have a problem understanding the capital accounts. Sometimes there is just one account called the capital account. In other cases, there may be several accounts: share capital account, revenue reserves account and so on.

What are the capital accounts?

The capital accounts represent the money invested in the business by the owners. If the company is wound up, and if the assets and liabilities are worth exactly book value, the owners will be paid out exactly the value of the capital accounts.

The owners of a business are a different entity from the business itself. This is easy to understand in the case of a listed public company. If you own shares in Barclays Bank plc, you are not the same as the bank. The capital accounts in the books of Barclays Bank plc represent the debt owing to you and to the other shareholders.

The principle is exactly the same in the accounts of a one-man or one-woman business. Let us return to Bridget Murphy, the public relations consultant. Bridget Murphy the person is separate from Bridget Murphy the business. If she is efficient, she will have two bank accounts, one for her business and one for her personal affairs. She may even pay herself a 'salary' from one bank account to the other.

If Bridget Murphy's business is wound up, what is left after everything has been collected in and paid out belongs to her. The final cheque in the cheque book pays her the value of the capital accounts.

This is the reason that the capital accounts are listed with the liabilities.

The layout of the balance sheet

Until the 1950s, it was the practice to set out the figures on a balance sheet side by side. The liabilities (credit balances) were listed in the left-hand column, and the assets (debit balances) were listed in the right-hand column. The two columns, of course, added up to the same figure.

You will almost certainly never see a balance sheet set out like this as it is now just about universally the practice to set out balance sheets in a vertical format. The examples in this chapter are set out in this way.

A vertical balance sheet shows liabilities deducted from assets in a logical manner. The whole thing adds down to the net worth of the business, which is shown at the bottom. This 'net worth' is represented by the capital accounts.

This is best illustrated with an example. The balance sheet of a partnership where the two partners participate 50/50 in the profits is shown below.

Smith and Jones
Balance sheet at 30 April 2015

	£	£
Fixed assets		
Freehold property	200,000	
Plant and machinery	120,000	
Motor vehicles	40,000	
		360,000
Current assets		
Stock	170,000	
Trade debtors	130,000	
	300,000	
Less current liabilities		
Bank overdraft	60,000	
Trade creditors	120,000	
	180,000	
Net current assets		120,000
		480,000
Capital accounts		
Smith		240,000
Jones		240,000
		480,000

This is, of course, a simple balance sheet. In practice, there would be several notes giving relevant details of how the figures are made up. Note that the net worth of the partnership is £480,000. If the partnership were to be wound up, if the assets and liabilities achieved exactly book value, and if there were no winding-up expenses, Smith and Jones would get £240,000 each.

Test your understanding

Now prepare a balance sheet from the trial balance given below. The answer is given at the end of today's work, but prepare your answer before checking. The accounts are given in alphabetical order, not the order in which they appear in the balance sheet.

John Cohen
Trial balance at 30 April 2015

	Debit £	Credit £
Bank account	10,000	
Capital reserve		70,000
Depreciation on motor vehicle		30,000
Depreciation on plant and machinery		140,000
Leasehold property	100,000	
Motor vehicles	60,000	
Plant and machinery	280,000	
Revenue reserves		240,000
Stock	150,000	
Taxation		80,000
Trade creditors		200,000
Trade debtors	160,000	
	760,000	760,000

Taxation is money owing to the government by the business. Depreciation must be netted off against the relevant asset accounts. This means that the difference between the two figures is shown in the balance sheet.

The main balance sheet headings

Of course, not every individual account in the trial balance appears individually in the balance sheet. If it did, the balance sheet of a major company would have to be hundreds of pages long. The need for this is overcome by grouping accounts of a similar type. For example, there may be several bank accounts but they will appear in the balance sheet as just one total figure.

The following explanations will help you understand the headings commonly used in balance sheets.

Fixed assets

These are assets whose use generates benefit to the business in the long term. This is usually taken to mean a year or more. Because of their fixed and long-term nature, they are grouped separately from current assets, whose value can be expected to be realized in the short term.

It is normally necessary to depreciate fixed assets – this was studied in detail earlier in the week. In practice, it is rare for fixed assets to be actually worth exactly their written down value in the books, for several reasons:

- the arbitrary nature of the depreciation rules
- individual circumstances
- inflation.

Examples of fixed assets are:

- freehold property
- leasehold property
- plant and equipment
- computers
- fixtures and fittings
- motor vehicles.

Asset strippers specialize in finding companies where the fixed assets are actually worth more than the book value. They then purchase the company and unlock the value by selling some or all of the assets and realizing the profit.

Current assets

These are assets whose value is available to the business immediately (such as cash) or in the short term. This is either because they are part of the trading cycle (such as stock and trade debtors) or because they are short-term investments (such as a 90-day bank deposit account). The definition of 'short term' is usually taken to be less than a year.

Debtors are usually current assets. The definition of a debtor is a person owing money to the business, such as a customer for goods sold. Examples of current assets are:

- stock
- trade debtors
- bank accounts
- short-term investments.

Current liabilities

These are liabilities that the business could be called upon to pay off in the short term. Examples are:

- trade creditors
- bank overdrafts
- taxation payable within one year
- hire purchase payable within one year.

The definition of a creditor is a person to whom the business owes money, such as a supplier.

Net current assets

This is also known as **working capital** and it is extremely important. It is the difference between current assets and current liabilities, and it can be a negative figure if the liabilities are greater.

It is extremely important because net current assets are what are available to finance the day-to-day running of the business. If net current assets are insufficient for this purpose, the business may have to close or seek some other form of finance. It is possible for a business to be profitable but have to close due to a shortage of working capital. It is relatively common for a business to be profitable but nonetheless embarrassed by a shortage of working capital.

Long-term liabilities

The John Cohen example above did not include one, but long-term liabilities are liabilities that are payable after more than a year. An example is a **fixed-term bank loan**. A business may be able to solve the problem of a shortage of working capital by obtaining a long-term liability in place of a bank overdraft.

Bank overdrafts are invariably legally repayable on demand. This means in theory, and very occasionally in practice, that the bank manager can demand repayment at 3 p.m. and, if payment has not been received, take steps to appoint an administrator or receiver at 4 p.m. On the other hand, a long-term fixed loan is repayable only when stipulated by the agreement and according to the conditions in the agreement.

Let us consider a ten-year loan of £1,000,000, repayable by ten equal annual instalments of £100,000. The balance sheet would show £900,000 under long-term liabilities and £100,000 under current liabilities. After a year, and one repayment, the balance sheet would show £800,000 under long-term liabilities and £100,000 under current liabilities. Hire purchase contract balances are split in the same way. The part repayable after a year is shown in long-term liabilities.

> ## Solving a shortage of working capital
>
> A business has an obvious incentive to make as many as possible of its liabilities long-term liabilities. This eases the pressure on working capital.

Summary

Today we have studied the remaining concepts you will need to know about before you can gain an understanding of published accounts. You have seen how accounts are prepared from basic bookkeeping records. You have learned:

- exactly what a balance sheet is
- how ownership is shown in the accounts
- how balance sheets are laid out
- how to prepare a balance sheet
- the meaning of the main balance sheet headings.

Tomorrow we will round off the week by studying the information provided in published accounts.

Test your understanding

Answers

John Cohen

SUNDAY

MONDAY

TUESDAY

WEDNESDAY

THURSDAY

FRIDAY

SATURDAY

	John Cohen	
	Balance sheet at 30 April 2015	
	£	£
Fixed assets		
Leasehold property	100,000	
Plant and machinery	140,000	
Motor vehicles	30,000	
		270,000
Current assets		
Stock	150,000	
Trade debtors	160,000	
Bank	10,000	
	320,000	
Less current liabilities		
Trade creditors	200,000	
Taxation	80,000	
	280,000	
Net current assets		40,000
		310,000
Capital		
Capital reserve	70,000	
Revenue reserve	240,000	
		310,000

Fact-check (answers at the back)

1. Why does the balance sheet balance, even though not all the balances in the trial balance are included?
a) It is not always the case that the balance sheet must balance ❏
b) It is because the balancing figure is included with the assets ❏
c) It is because the balancing figure is included with the liabilities ❏
d) It is because the net profit or loss is added to (or subtracted from) the capital accounts ❏

2. What is the state of the capital accounts?
a) Always credit ❏
b) Usually credit ❏
c) Usually debit ❏
d) Always debit ❏

3. What does it mean if the capital accounts of a company add up to a net debit balance?
a) The business is insolvent and needs an injection of capital ❏
b) The shareholders are required by law to buy more shares ❏
c) The shareholders are required by law to loan money to the company ❏
d) Shareholders are required to repay past dividends ❏

4. Total assets less total liabilities equals what?
a) The working capital ❏
b) The share capital ❏
c) The net worth of the business ❏
d) The non-current liabilities ❏

5. What is normally first shown in a balance sheet?
a) Capital ❏
b) Current assets ❏
c) Fixed assets ❏
d) Working capital ❏

6. Where does stock go in a balance sheet?
a) In fixed assets ❏
b) In current assets ❏
c) In current liabilities ❏
d) In long-term liabilities ❏

7. How short term must a liability be in order for it to be classed as a current liability?
a) Payable within a month ❏
b) Payable within six months ❏
c) Payable within a year ❏
d) Payable within two years ❏

8. Debtors are usually what?
a) Current assets ❏
b) Current liabilities ❏
c) Long-term liabilities ❏
d) Capital ❏

9. Is it possible for a business to be profitable but to be short of working capital?
a) Yes, and it is relatively common ❑
b) Yes, but it is very unlikely ❑
c) No, it is not possible ❑
d) The question is self-evidently absurd ❑

10. A company borrows £300,000 from a bank. It is a long-term loan repayable in equal monthly instalments over five years. How much of this will be classed as a current liability in a balance sheet three years later?
a) £300,000 ❑
b) Nothing ❑
c) £120,000 ❑
d) £60,000 ❑

Understanding published accounts

Today we will be studying the content and layout of published accounts. Companies are obliged by law to publish their accounts, and it will be helpful if you obtain a set of such accounts to refer to. The accounts will be particularly useful if they are for a company well known to you, such as your employer.

A study of published accounts cannot help but be interesting and useful. Firstly, it will help you understand your investments and help you decide whether to buy or sell. Even if you think that you do not have investments, it is highly likely that you do, perhaps through a pension fund or a share-based ISA. Secondly, it can help you judge the security of your employer or prospective employer.

Published accounts, of course, have many other uses and, short of fraud, much information must be disclosed and cannot be hidden.

Today's programme is perhaps the most demanding of the week. It looks at:

- availability of published accounts and how to obtain them
- what has to be included
- profit and loss account and balance sheet
- the remainder of the annual report and accounts.

Availability of published accounts

Accounts are published for one or both of the following reasons:

- because it is required by law
- as a public relations exercise.

All but a tiny number of registered UK companies are required by law to produce accounts annually, although, subject to strict limits, the period can be changed. In many cases an audit is required. A private company must file accounts at Companies House within nine months of the balance sheet date and a public company must do so within six months of the balance sheet date. An extension of the filing period may be allowed in rare and exceptional cases. The law and accounting standards stipulate the minimum content and standard of the accounts.

'Remember that credit is money.'

Benjamin Franklin

Certain bodies other than companies are also required to produce accounts. Examples are building societies, charities and local authorities. Our work today deals exclusively with the accounts of companies.

> ## Companies House
>
> The address for companies registered in England and Wales is Companies House, Cardiff CF14 3UZ. There is an office in Edinburgh for companies registered in Scotland and an office in Belfast for companies registered in Northern Ireland. The telephone number for all three offices is 0303 1234 500 and the website for all three is www.gov.uk/government/organisations/companies-house. There are over 3,200,000 live companies on the register and the accounts of all but a handful of them may be inspected.

How to obtain published accounts

A listed public company will probably be willing to make accounts available. A request should be made to the Company Secretary's department.

Alternatively, you can obtain a copy of the accounts of any company, even the corner shop, by applying to Companies House. You can also get a copy of the company's annual return, articles and other documents. You will need to give the company's exact registered name or its registered number or preferably both. You can telephone and have the document posted to you or arrange it through the website. There is a small charge of £3 per document. You can pay with a credit or debit card.

It may be useful and particularly interesting if you look at the accounts of your employer or another company that you know well.

Late filing

Unfortunately, a small minority of companies file their accounts late or even not at all. This is an offence for which the directors can be punished and the company can incur a penalty, but it does happen. It is often companies with problems that file late.

What is included

The content of the annual report and accounts is governed by the law and **accounting standards**, although directors do still have some discretion. Listed companies are required to use international accounting standards; other companies can use international accounting standards or UK accounting standards. However, once international standards have been used, a company can go back to UK standards only in exceptional circumstances. The presentation of the accounts and the figures shown will differ according to the set of accounting standards used.

If you are looking at the report and accounts of a listed company, you will see the following:

- Independent auditor's report
- Balance sheet (or it might be called Statement of financial position)
- Statement of comprehensive income (or it might be called Income statement). This corresponds with the profit and loss account
- Statement of changes in equity
- Statement of cash flows
- Notes to the financial statements
- Chairman's statement
- Directors' report
- Business review
- Directors' remuneration report.

If the company is using UK standards, the financial information will comprise the following:

- Balance sheet
- Profit and loss account
- Statement of total recognized gains and losses
- Cash flow statement (probably)
- Notes to the financial statements.

Reports will be filed with this financial information.

For accounts periods starting from 1 January 2016 (January 2015 at directors' option) medium-sized companies (up to £36,000,000 turnover, subject to conditions) and small companies (up to £10,200,000, subject to conditions) may file still less detail. Subject to conditions, an audit is not required for small companies.

Finding your way around published accounts

Space here is limited and there is so much detail that there is really no substitute for diving in and having a look at the report and accounts of your chosen company. Try not to get bogged down! Assuming that you are not looking at the report and accounts of a small or medium-sized company and assuming that the company uses UK accounting standards, can you find out the following?

1 The pre-tax profit (profit and loss account)
2 Details of the fixed assets (balance sheet and supporting notes)
3 The amount of any exports (the notes)
4 Whether it is an unqualified audit report (auditor's report)
5 Details of any political or charitable donation (directors' report)
6 Whether there was a cash outflow in the period (cash flow statement)
7 Details of the share capital (balance sheet and supporting notes)
8 The amount of the capital employed (balance sheet).

Profit and loss account and balance sheet

As we have seen earlier this week, these are the core of the accounts, and we have already looked at some of the principles. The profit and loss account will give the figures for the previous period as well as the current period. Figures in the balance sheet will be given as at the previous balance sheet date as well as for the present one.

Now we will have a look at what will be shown in the published profit and loss account and balance sheet of a company. Once again, UK accounting standards are assumed. Some of the information may be given in notes with a suitable cross-reference.

The profit and loss account

Most people consider that the key figure is the one for profit before tax. You may think that taxation is fair, or at any rate inevitable, and that profit before tax is the best measure of a company's success.

The bottom part of the profit and loss account will look rather like this example. Fictitious figures have been inserted here.

P&L account

Profit before tax	£10,000,000
Less Tax on profit	£3,200,000
Profit for the year	£6,800,000
Less Dividends paid and proposed	£4,000,000
Retained profit for the year	£2,800,000
Retained profit brought forward	£7,000,000
Retained profit carried forward	£9,800,000

In this example the Government is taking £3,200,000 of the profit as tax and £4,000,000 is being distributed to shareholders. The company started the current period with undistributed profits of £7,000,000 and it is prudently adding £2,800,000 to this figure. Undistributed profits are now £9,800,000 and this figure will appear in the balance sheet.

The profit and loss account will give the **turnover**, which is the total invoiced sales in the period. This is very important and it is useful to work out the relationship between the profit and the turnover.

The balance sheet

Fixed assets

These are normally the first item appearing in the balance sheet. You will usually see just one figure for the net amount of the fixed assets and a cross-reference to a note. This note will:

1 break down the assets by type
2 give cumulative expenditure for each type
3 give cumulative depreciation for each type
4 give net asset value for each type (2 minus 3)
5 state the depreciation policy for each type.

The fixed assets are usually one of the most interesting sections of the accounts. This is because it is rare for the assets to be worth exactly the figure shown.

Depreciation according to accounting rules rarely reflects the real-life situation, especially in times of inflation. One wonders what the book value of St Paul's Cathedral would be if the Church of England had followed depreciation rules at the time of Sir Christopher Wren.

In practice, companies sometimes revalue property assets though not usually other assets. Asset strippers specialize in buying undervalued companies then selling the fixed assets for more than book value. This is one of the reasons why the details, which will be in the notes, are so important.

Current assets and current liabilities
First, the current assets will be listed by type and a total of the current assets will be given. Then the current liabilities will be listed by type and the total of the current liabilities will be given.

The difference between the two figures will be stated and this is the *net current assets* or the *working capital*. A problem is usually indicated if the current assets are smaller or only slightly larger than the current liabilities.

The assets and liabilities will be cross-referenced to notes giving appropriate details such as:

- a breakdown of stocks into finished goods and work in progress
- a split of debtors between trade debtors (customers) and other debtors
- details of the different types of creditors.

Capital and reserves
On Friday we examined the net worth of an organization shown at the bottom of its balance sheet. This section is the net worth of the company.

If the company were to be solvent and wound up, ignoring the costs of the winding up and in the unlikely event of all the assets and liabilities realizing exact book value, the total of this section is the amount that would be distributed to shareholders.

A note will give details of the different types of share capital if there is more than one. It will also give the figures for the different types of reserves, and the retained figure in the profit and loss account.

The remainder of the annual report and accounts

You will find that published accounts also include additional notes, the directors' report, the cash flow statement, the auditor's report and the consolidated accounts where appropriate.

Notes to the accounts

There are always notes to the profit and loss account and balance sheet. Their purpose is to give further details, and they are in the form of notes to prevent the accounts from becoming too detailed and complicated. Many of the notes give a breakdown of such figures as stock and debtors.

The notes also state the accounting policies and conventions used in the preparation of the accounts. These are extremely important because these policies can greatly affect the figures. An example of such a policy would be to value stocks at cost or net realizable value, whichever is lower. Any change to this policy could greatly affect the profit figure.

The directors' report

The directors are required by law to provide certain information. This includes, for example, the amount of directors' remuneration and details of any political or charitable contributions. This information is disclosed in the directors' report.

Cash flow statement

There are sometimes disputes about the figures in the profit and loss account and balance sheet. This is one reason why cash is so important. Cash is much more a matter of fact than opinion. It is either there or it is not there.

Where the cash came from (banks, shareholders, customers) is also a matter of fact. So, too, is where the cash went to (dividends, wages, suppliers, etc.). The statement gives all this information.

The auditor's report

The law requires company accounts to be audited. The auditor must be a person or firm holding one of the approved qualifications.

For accounts periods starting from 1 January 2016, subject to conditions no audit is required if annual turnover is less than £10,200,000. The auditors will state whether in their opinion the accounts give a true and fair view. They do not certify the accuracy of the figures, a point that is often misunderstood.

If the auditors have reservations, they will give reasons for their concern. Serious qualifications are rare, partly because it is in the interests of directors that they are avoided. Technical and less serious qualifications are more common. It is a matter of judgement how seriously each one is regarded.

Consolidated accounts

If a company is part of a group of companies, it needs to include consolidated accounts. A large group may comprise a hundred or more companies, and it would obviously give an incomplete picture if each of these companies gave information just about its own activities. This is especially true when companies in a group trade with one another.

This is why the holding company must include consolidated accounts as well as its own figures. The effect of inter-group trading is eliminated and the consolidated balance sheet gives the group's position in relation to the outside world. This does not, however, remove the obligation for every group company to prepare and file its own accounts. Such accounts must include the name, in the opinion of the directors, of the ultimate holding company.

Summary

Today we have rounded off our introduction to bookkeeping and accounting by looking at published accounts in detail. We have:

- examined the obligation to publish accounts and seen where copies can be obtained
- seen what is included in a company's annual report and accounts
- tested our knowledge
- conducted an outline study of the annual report and accounts.

By now you should be able to look at a set of accounts and understand just what they contain. You should be able to decipher what the different columns of figures mean and have a firm grasp of all the basic terms and definitions used in accounting.

It is worth keeping this guide to hand so that you can revisit any sections of the book that you did not quite understand at the time. When learning anything new, progress requires a solid base on which to build. Good luck!

Fact-check (answers at the back)

1. How long from the balance sheet date is allowed for a private registered company to send its statutory accounts to Companies House?
   a) Three months ❏
   b) Six months ❏
   c) Nine months ❏
   d) One year ❏

2. Where is Companies House for companies registered in England and Wales?
   a) London ❏
   b) Cardiff ❏
   c) Norwich ❏
   d) Budleigh Salterton ❏

3. How much does Companies House charge for providing a document in paper form?
   a) £1 ❏
   b) £3 ❏
   c) £5 ❏
   d) £10 ❏

4. Must sole traders provide accounts to Companies House?
   a) Yes ❏
   b) No ❏
   c) Only if turnover is more than £10,000,000 ❏
   d) Only if net assets are more than £1,000,000 ❏

5. What is the turnover limit (subject to conditions) for filing abbreviated accounts for medium-sized companies at Companies House?
   a) £6,500,000 ❏
   b) £6,900,000 ❏
   c) £25,000,000 ❏
   d) £36,000,000 ❏

6. Which document discloses the net worth of a company?
   a) Balance sheet ❏
   b) Profit and loss account ❏
   c) Directors' report ❏
   d) Statement of cash flows ❏

7. What is the difference between the figures for current assets and current liabilities?
   a) Net current assets or working capital ❏
   b) Net cash flow ❏
   c) Shareholders' funds ❏
   d) Free capital ❏

8. In the case of a private company where would you find details of directors' remuneration?
   a) Balance sheet ❏
   b) Profit and loss account ❏
   c) Directors' report ❏
   d) Audit report ❏

9. Which of the following is given in the notes to the accounts?
   a) The figure for working capital ❏
   b) Comparative figures for the previous period ❏
   c) The names of the directors ❏
   d) Accounting policies used ❏

10. How many companies in the UK send accounts to Companies House?
   a) Fewer than 50,000 ❏
   b) Just over 500,000 ❏
   c) Just over 3,200,000 ❏
   d) More than 5,000,000 ❏

7 × 7

Seven things to do regularly

1 Do the bank reconciliation and investigate any discrepancies.

2 Do other relevant reconciliations and take any necessary action.

3 Consider the adequacy of the bad debt reserve. If it is too big or too small, it will affect the profit.

4 If relevant, consider the stock reserve (for lost, damaged, obsolete stock etc.). If it is too big or too small, the profit will be affected.

5 Remind yourself of the significance of GIGO, which stands for 'garbage in equals garbage out'. Your computer does not have a brain and any mistakes in the input will affect the information produced.

6 Sort out any suspense accounts in the accounting system.

7 Check the petty cash.

Seven things to remember

1 A profit and loss account summarizes activity over a period of time. The period must be stated.

2 A balance sheet summarizes assets and liabilities as at a specified date. The date must be stated.

3 There are only self-imposed rules for unpublished accounts prepared for management purposes. Published accounts must conform with the law and applicable accounting standards.

4 A change in accounting policies (the rules for depreciation, for example) will result in a change in the accounts figures. Details of any such change should be stated.

5 The net worth of a business is shown as a liability in the balance sheet. This is because it is owing to the owners, who are separate from the business.

6 Profits should be recognized when they have been earned. Losses should be recognized when they can be realistically foreseen.

7 Despite the rather cruel jokes, accountants are generally very nice people.

Seven golden rules

1 Double-entry bookkeeping is superior to single-entry bookkeeping.

2 If you keep manual records (which is probably unlikely), it is debit on the left and credit on the right.

3 For every debit there must be a credit.

4 The sum of all the credits must equal the sum of all the debits.

5 The principles of bookkeeping are timeless. Computers do exactly what can be done manually, but they do it more quickly and efficiently, and they probably present the end results in a different way.

6 You very probably will not get accurate accounts unless you have accurate accruals and prepayments.

7 The profit and loss account is a summary of all the revenue and expense balances. The balance sheet is a summary of all the assets and liabilities.

Seven things to avoid

1 Putting income accounts and expenditure accounts in the balance sheet.

2 Putting asset and liability accounts in the profit and loss account.

3 Not having a logical numbering system for the individual accounts.

4 Not keeping the bank reconciliation and other reconciliations up to date.

5 Not taking sufficient care with the accruals and prepayments. This may result in the profit being overstated or understated.

6 Not taking sufficient care with the reserves and provisions. An inadequate reserve (for bad debts, for example) will cause the profit to be overstated.

7 Forgetting that the period of the profit and loss account must be stated and that the chosen period can make a difference. This is particularly the case if seasonal goods are sold.

Seven trends for tomorrow

The following trends are all discernible now. They are likely to continue.

1 People will continue to question the value of the statutory audit.

2 Basic bookkeeping will continue to be subcontracted to countries that pay low wages.

3 There will continue to be accounting scandals.

4 Accounting standards will continue to develop.

5 Accounting software will become even more sophisticated.

6 Suppliers, customers, the government and others will increasingly demand that businesses communicate with them electronically. This affects tax returns, payment procedures, etc.

7 Managers and employees will increasingly be expected to have some knowledge of the principles of bookkeeping and accounts.

Seven great quotes

1 'The lack of money is the root of all evil.' Mark Twain (1835–1920), American writer

2 'When I was young I thought that money was the most important thing in life; now that I am old I know that it is.' Oscar Wilde (1854–1900), Irish writer

3 'Few have heard of Fra Luca Pacioli, the inventor of double-entry bookkeeping, but he has probably had more influence on human life than has Dante or Michelangelo.' Herbert J. Muller (1905–80), American historian

4 'Accountants are the witch-doctors of the modern world and willing to turn their hands to any kind of magic.' Charles Eustace Harman (1894–1970), British judge

5 'Civilization and profits go hand in hand.' Calvin Coolidge (1872–1933), American president

6 'Lenin was right. There is no subtler, no surer means of overturning the existing basis of society than to debauch the currency.' John Maynard Keynes (1883–1946), English economist

7 'No one would remember the Good Samaritan if he'd only had good intentions. He had money as well.' Margaret Thatcher (1925–2013), British prime minister

Seven great jokes*

1 If an accountant's wife cannot sleep, what does she say? 'Darling, could you tell me about your work?'

2 When does a person decide to become an accountant? When he realizes he doesn't have the charisma to succeed as an undertaker.

3 There are three types of accountant – those who can count and those who can't.

4 Why don't old accountants ever die? They just lose their balance.

5 How do you know when you've found a good accountant? She has a tax loophole named after her.

6 What's the definition of an auditor? Someone who goes on to the battlefield after the battle and bayonets the survivors.

7 What's the definition of an accountant? Someone who solves a problem you didn't know you had in a way that you don't understand.

---

* The writer is an accountant.

Glossary

account A section of the financial records listing transactions of the same type.

accounts A set of documents summarizing the financial transactions during a period and the position at the end of the period.

accruals Costs incurred but not yet entered into the financial records.

asset Something owned that has a value (e.g. a motor vehicle and money in a bank account).

asset account An account recording a particular type of asset.

audit An inspection and review of the financial transactions and accounts.

bad debt Money owing to the business or other organization that cannot be recovered.

balance sheet A summary of assets and liabilities at a stated date. The total of each must be the same figure.

books A set of accounts.

book value The value of an asset as recorded in the accounts. It may or may not be the same as the actual value.

capital The amount by which the assets exceed the liabilities. It is the 'net worth' of the organization.

capital account An account showing the amount invested in a business by its owners (e.g. share capital, revenue reserves).

cash book A record of money paid out and received.

consolidated accounts A set of accounts showing the overall position of a group of companies. Inter-group trading and debts are eliminated.

creditor Person or business to whom money is owed (e.g. an unpaid supplier).

current assets Cash and assets expected to be turned into cash in the short term, usually taken to be within a year (e.g. stock).

current liabilities Liabilities payable in the short term, usually taken to be within a year.

debtor A person or business owing money to the business (e.g. a customer who has not paid for goods supplied).

depreciation The reduction in the value of a fixed asset over a period of time (e.g. due to wear and tear).

double-entry bookkeeping A method of bookkeeping in which each transaction is recorded twice, once as a debit and once as a credit.

expenditure Amount of money paid out.

expenditure account An account listing expenditure of a profit and loss nature.

fixed assets Assets intended to be held for the long term, usually taken to be more than a year.

holding company A company that owns a total or major share in at least one subsidiary company.

income Total sales and other income credited over a period.

income account An account showing sales credited or other income over a period.

insolvent A situation where liabilities are greater than assets.

invoice A demand (more politely, a request) for payment for goods or services.

journal A posting medium that is used for transactions not recorded in any of the other books of entry.

ledger A book or loose-leaf collection of all the accounts in the system. It is frequently held in computerized form.

liability Money owing by the organization (e.g. a bank overdraft or money owing to a supplier).

liability account An account recording a particular type of liability.

long-term liability A debt due for payment after a period of a year.

market value The realizable value of an asset. It may or may not be the same as the book value.

nominal ledger The principal ledger. Other ledgers are subsidiary to it.

opening balance The first balance in an accounting period brought forward from the closing balance in the previous period.

overheads The costs (other than direct costs such as the cost of goods sold) of running a business.

petty cash A small cash float that can be drawn on for small items of expenditure.

profit The amount remaining when all costs have been deducted from the total of all the income.

profit and loss account A summary of the income and expenditure accounts, showing income and expenditure in a stated period, and hence the profit or loss.

provisions Reserves created to cover claims that may or will definitely be made against the organization in the future (e.g. warranty claims and potential legal disputes).

reconciliation Identification of the reasons for differences between figures (e.g. bank reconciliation). It may lead to corrections being made.

reserves A term virtually interchangeable with 'provisions' – money set aside to settle definite or possible claims. It can also mean a section of the capital accounts reflecting the net worth of the business (e.g. revenue reserve).

revenue The total of accounts of an income nature.

single-entry bookkeeping A method of bookkeeping in which each item is entered only once. It is inferior to double-entry bookkeeping.

solvent A situation where assets are greater than liabilities

stock Goods for sale held by a business.

suspense account An account in which accounting entries are temporarily placed, before they are allocated to the correct, permanent place.

trial balance A listing of all the balances in a double-entry bookkeeping system. The total of the debits must equal the total of the credits.

turnover Invoiced sales and other income in a stated period.

working capital The amount by which current assets exceeds current liabilities.

Answers

Sunday: 1a; 2c; 3d; 4b; 5c; 6c; 7c; 8b; 9c; 10a.

Monday: 1b; 2c; 3b and c; 4a; 5b; 6d; 7a; 8a; 9d; 10d.

Tuesday: 1b; 2a; 3b; 4d; 5d; 6c; 7b; 8a; 9c; 10d.

Wednesday: 1b; 2b; 3a; 4c; 5c; 6d (this is because it is necessary to reduce the bad debt reserve account which has a credit balance); 7d; 8c; 9d; 10a.

Thursday: 1c; 2b; 3a; 4d; 5b; 6d; 7b; 8c; 9d; 10a.

Friday: 1d; 2b; 3a; 4c; 5c; 6b; 7c; 8a; 9a; 10d.

Saturday: 1c; 2b; 3b; 4b; 5d; 6a; 7a; 8c; 9d; 10c.